A Trip Around the World

25 patchwork, quilting and appliqué
projects inspired by different countries

GAIL LAWTHER

GUILD OF MASTER CRAFTSMAN PUBLICATIONS LTD

Welcome to
A Trip Around the World!

Quite a few years ago, my husband Chris and I sat down with a map and planned a trip round the world. We had friends in all kinds of far-flung places, and we longed to visit them and see the wonderful countries they lived in. We planned a trip that included Australia, New Zealand, Thailand, Israel and Trinidad (among plenty of other places!); the lack of direct flights from Israel to Bangkok looked as though it might present a problem, but we were sure that we'd find a way around it.

There was, of course, only one problem; we didn't have anything approaching the funds to do such a trip. Since then the friends who lived in Bangkok have come back to Southampton; the ones who were in Israel now live near us on the south coast. In the meantime, though, we've had some fantastic opportunities to visit places that weren't even on our original itinerary, and explored some of the wonders of the world – it's just that we've done it in bits, rather than in one adventure.

So, instead, we've decided to make our trip around the world in the form of this book – a celebration of the places we've had the chance to visit so far, and an imaginary trip to the parts of the globe that are beyond our present horizons. Sit back and enjoy the journey with us!

The Trip

Every part of the world abounds in wonderful source material for quilters and other stitchers. Decorative patterns; motifs carved in wood or stone; designs woven or stitched into textiles, or painted onto porcelain or walls – everywhere you look there's a wealth of pattern, texture and colour. Sometimes people ask me where I get my ideas from, and my answer is always the same: everywhere. Maybe I have a particularly fertile brain for pattern and design, but everywhere I look I see inspiration. A wrought iron railing; a design hammered in nails into a wooden door; the veins in a leaf or the coloured spots in the centre of a flower; the ripples on a river or the reflections in a stagnant pond. I once even made a sketch of the design stamped into the edge of a paper napkin before the waiter came and removed it (the napkin, not the sketch …).

My aim in this book is to take inspiration for patchwork, quilting and appliqué projects from different countries around the world. Of course, in every region of the world there's so much decorative detail and so many traditional patterns that a book like this can only be a sampler – just as a real trip around the world leaves as many places out as it includes! For the book's global tour I've started our journey in North America and Canada, then hopped and skipped around the globe in a westerly direction, ending up in my home territory, the British Isles.

For every section of the world covered, I've researched decorative patterns of the area, building some of these into projects, and including others in the pattern library pages.

The Projects

For the main projects, I've chosen representative motifs or designs or techniques from the area being visited, and built these into one or more projects which you can easily reproduce. Each project has full instructions, including step-by-step diagrams where necessary, plus templates or trace-offs. Wherever it's practical I've included the templates at full size; where the project is too large, you'll find a complete pattern with instructions on how to enlarge it to the required size.

The projects vary in difficulty from the extremely simple to the quite challenging. Before the materials list in each one I've given a 'stitching guide'; this tells you how easy or complex the project is and if there are any particular skills that will be useful when you're working it, eg basic rotary cutting skills. The materials list tells you what I used to make the project in that particular colour-scheme, and at that specific size, but of course every project can be worked in different colours and/or techniques to suit your own preferences.

The Pattern Libraries

For each region of the world I've also included one or more pattern library pages. These pages contain extra motifs from the region that you can develop and combine in your own designs. On pages 9-13 you'll find suggestions for different ways in which you can develop motifs by combining them in numerous different ways, then stitching them in a wide variety of patchwork, quilting and appliqué techniques. It's astonishing how much you can vary the appearance of one simple motif just by using different types of stitching and embellishment to produce the design. And, if these designs give you a taste for experimentation, I've included a book list on page 112 – this includes several titles that explore the ornamentation and decorative motifs of various countries.

Looking around

One of the secrets of good design is knowing how to look. Maybe this seems a strange concept to you – surely either we see something or we don't? But looking in depth means seeing the potential of a shape, a scene, a texture, a combination of colours or lines. On these pages I want us to take a look together at an ordinary scene and then see how we could use different parts of it as springboards for textile ideas. You don't have to be good at drawing to expand some of these ideas, but it really does help to take a sketchbook or a camera when you go anywhere that might prove inspirational – then you can jot down ideas, a tiny part of a pattern, notes on a particular colour-scheme etc.

The scenario …

Here we are (above) in one of the main squares in Ravenna, Italy. Ravenna's famous for its fabulous 5th century mosaics, but many other aspects of the town are inspirational for designers too. This square is a wonderful mixture of old and new; many of the buildings are mediaeval – including the one at the far end which houses a surprising franchise. Yes, it's the Ravenna MacDonalds!

A quick glance around the square gives an overall impression of space, broken up into attractive buildings round the edges, lit by a warm Mediterranean light. For me, the inspiration begins here; what sense of colour and texture does it give me? Can I capture this feel in fabrics, or in bits torn from magazines? Exercises like this can often be the starting point for textile projects. The selection of fabric swatches on the left echoes the colours and textures of the walls, the stonework and the light in the square.

Moving in closer …

In the other photographs on these pages I've focused more closely on buildings and attractive details around the square, and overleaf you'll find a selection of quilting motifs I've developed from these details.

The details

Here are some motifs I've developed from the photographs of Ravenna. The border design (**a**) is from the wrought iron balcony, and the stone capital has been turned into a foliage motif (**b**). I've developed the outline of the stone plaque on page 6 into shield-shaped border (**c**), and the wrought iron above the doorway makes a superb segmented design (**d**). Finally, two designs from the bottom of the fountain and one from a doorway make lovely medallions (**e**, **f** and **g**).

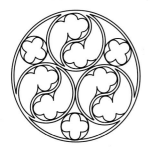

Developing patterns

Sometimes you'll come across a wonderful, complex design – a painted ceiling, perhaps, or one of the fabulous full-page decorations in a mediaeval manuscript. How do you begin to translate it into a workable design for quilting or appliqué? One of the tricks of strong design is to simplify.

Instead of trying to translate the whole design, lock stock and barrel, pick out one or two basic motifs. Simplify and stylise the shapes so that they're easy to handle, then try combining them in different ways. On this page I've included some examples of inspirational photographs, then picked a motif from a couple of them which could be built up into different designs – you'll find suggestions for ways of combining motifs on pages 10 and 11.

Adapting a basic shape

To illustrate this idea, I've chosen a curved shape (a) which appears in varying forms in the decorative motifs of many countries; the examples on this pages show just some of the ways in which it can be built up into different patterns.

Try the same idea with your own motifs. Draw your chosen shape at several different sizes, then cut it out of template plastic so that you can draw round it easily. Try drawing your shapes in rows, staggered, radiating out from the centre, overlapping, in stripes etc. If one design doesn't work, move on to another!

b A simple outline creates a strong single motif.

c This particular shape tessellates well – repeats fit into each other without leaving gaps.

d A double line echoes one edge of each individual shape.

e The same idea, this time echoing two edges of each shape.

f Overlapping motifs placed on their side create a secondary clamshell design.

g Repeats ripple out each side from a central pair.

h The two sides of the motifs have been separated and then outlined to create a continuous border.

i Small motifs are alternated with inverted repeats.

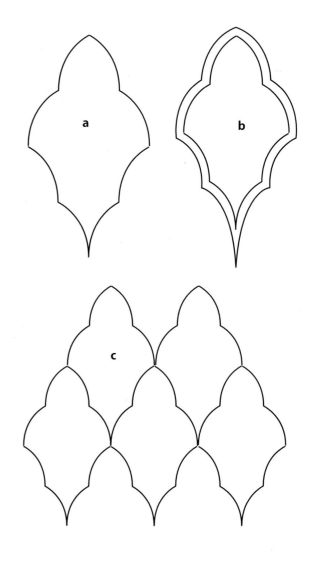

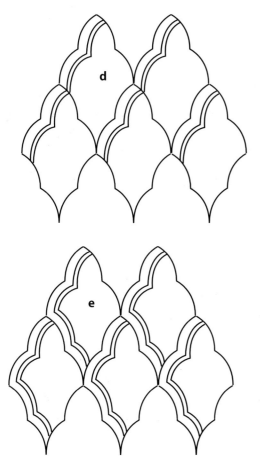

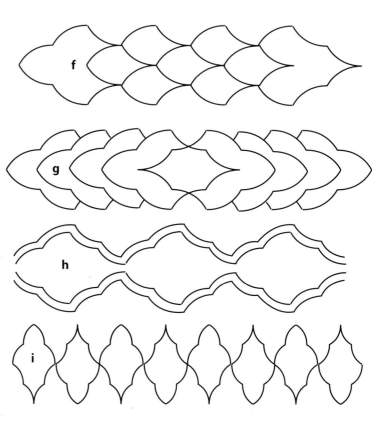

j, k, l *Small alternating repeats create secondary patterns between them.*

m *Another double line idea, this time deleting the right-hand sides of each motif.*

n, o *Four repeats create a simple medallion, used either square or 'on point.'*

p *Single line motifs overlap to produce secondary shapes.*

q *Six repeats radiating from a central point, overlapping each other and with an extra line echoing the outline.*

r *Outlined motifs are drawn to look as though they interlock.*

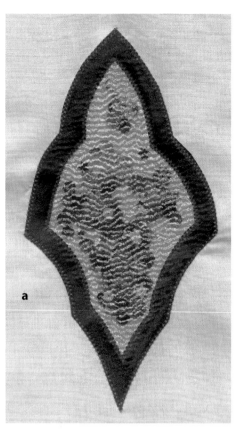

a

FOR THE EXAMPLES ON THESE PAGES, I've taken some of the strongest designs from my first experiments (see previous pages) and stitched them in varying ways. One of the ways of expanding your creativity is to try the same design out using different types of stitching; as well as ordinary quilting, try sashiko stitching, corded quilting, appliqué by hand and machine, reverse appliqué, machine quilting, fabric painting, Hawaiian appliqué etc. Vary the colours and textures of the fabrics and threads you use, and work the design at different sizes; it's astonishing how different the same design can appear depending on the way it's stitched.

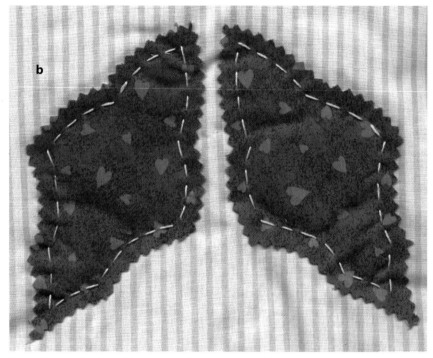

b

c

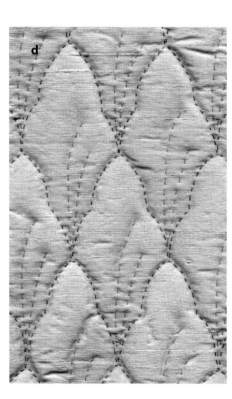

d

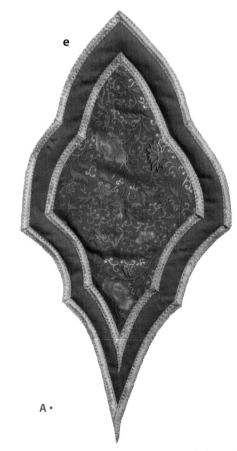

e

a A shadow-work motif with sequins trapped under sheer fabric

b Motifs cut with pinking shears and quilted with large running stitches

c Different-sized motifs cut in sheer fabrics

d Tessellated shapes stitched on silk

e Rich fabrics outlined in gold binding

f Medallion design in wholecloth quilting

g Rich fabrics fused with Appliglue

h Continuous design stitched by machine

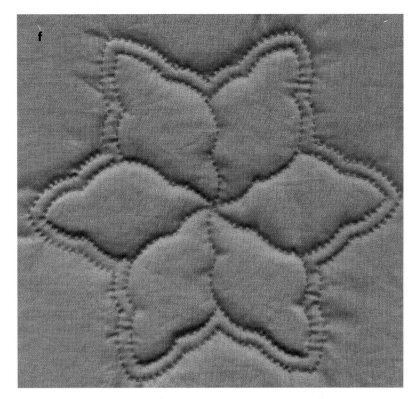

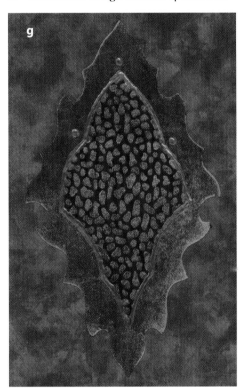

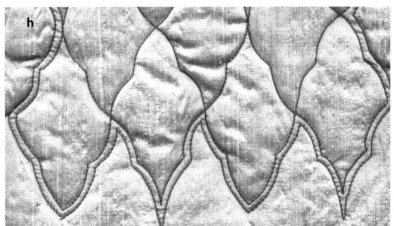

Let the fabric do some of the work, too; some fabrics just cry out to be used for particular countries!

General instructions

You don't really need any special skills to complete most of the projects in this book; within each project you'll find step-by-step instructions, plus clear line drawings illustrating different stages along the way. I'll just spell out a few basic instructions, though, which will help you along your way – particularly if you're new to quilting.

Equipment

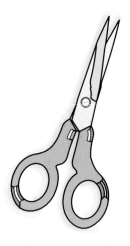

Your basic sewing kit will be adequate for most of the projects; I'll just add a few notes where they're helpful.

* needles in a variety of sizes
* pins (use large glass-headed or flower pins; they're easier on the fingers than conventional ones)
* sewing and tacking threads
* scissors (you'll need a small pair with sharp points, and a larger pair for cutting fabric shapes)
* thimble if you use one (particularly useful for quilting)
* tape measure

You'll also need paper, pencil, rubber, ruler and paper scissors for some of the projects; you'll find drawing tools listed under the materials when they're important.

There are many gadgets of different types which are sold specifically with quilters in mind; by all means use them if you find them useful, but don't feel you have to acquire them specially. Specialised items which often do come in handy are long and short quilters' rules, which are marked with all kinds of handy measurements, and a rotary cutter and self-healing board or mat. Template plastic is sometimes useful for creating small templates; it comes in sheets and is very cheap. Also, of course, a sewing machine will speed up many of the projects, although if you're totally committed to stitching by hand you can probably adapt them all to hand sewing.

Preparing fabrics

If the item you're making is something that you'll be laundering, pre-wash the fabrics first to get rid of any extra dye and finishing, and also to pre-shrink them. (If you won't be laundering the item, eg the fabrics for the boat picture on page 76, you don't need to pre-wash.) After washing, pull the grain of the fabric square, and press the fabric ready for cutting; if the fabric seems to have lost a bit of body during washing, give it a couple of sprays of spray starch while you're ironing it. This is also good preparation for any fabrics you're going to cut with a rotary cutter.

Templates

Wherever possible, the templates and patterns for the projects are included full-size. Occasionally they have to be enlarged; if it's by a

small amount I suggest doing the enlargement on a photocopier, which is more accurate than drawing them by eye. The instructions will give the percentage enlargement that you need. Where the pattern has to be drawn at a much larger scale, for instance the cat on page 24 or the mandarin ducks on page 40, I've included a grid across the drawing. The instructions on page 41 tell you how to use a grid for enlarging a design.

Try to cut as accurately as possible whenever you're using a template, and always remember to put the template right side up on the right side of your fabric; this is vital when the shape is asymmetrical, so it's a good habit to cultivate!

Measurements

Throughout the book I've given the measurements in metric and imperial; sometimes these aren't exact equivalents, so always work either in metric or in imperial throughout the project. Measurements for things such as fabric pieces needed for a project are just guidelines; you may have a scrap of fabric that's big enough even if it isn't a nice neat square or rectangle.

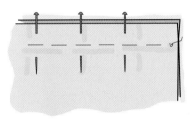

Seams

As a general rule, make your seams ¼in (5mm) wide unless I've specified something different. If it's helpful, stick a piece of masking tape on the needle plate of your machine to help you keep the seam straight and a constant width.

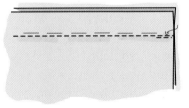

Pressing

When you're assembling patchwork, try and press your work after each seam you stitch – it may seem tedious, but it gives a much better result. Just set the iron up near your sewing machine, so that you can move easily from one to the other as necessary. Press seams either open, or to the darker sides, whichever you prefer. When you're working with metallic fabrics, try a little waste piece out first; use the iron as cool as possible, and cover the surface of the fabric with a protective layer of paper or fabric if necessary to prevent it from catching.

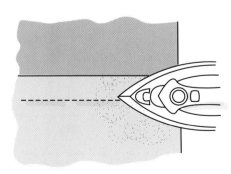

Making your quilt 'sandwich'

When you're quilting an item, there are various ways of keeping the three layers (top, wadding and backing) together as you stitch. The conventional method is by tacking, working horizontal and vertical lines of tacking at regular intervals across the project. Some quilters prefer to use safety pins across the quilt surface; others use tack guns which shoot little plastic tags through the layers. Still others use the special glue sold to quilters; I use this a lot, although I'm a little wary of spraying it on anything that might be used by a baby or an allergy sufferer; consult the manufacturers if in doubt. If the item is very small, just a few pins may be enough to hold the layers together while you quilt them. There are no rights and wrongs; just use whichever method you feel most comfortable with.

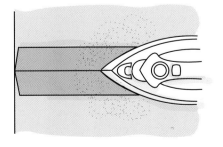

North America & Canada

Coming from the tiny British Isles, where the terrain alters drastically every 50 miles or so, I can still remember vividly the astonishing experiences of flying over hundreds of miles of pack-ice off Newfoundland, and seeing enormous wheatfields in North America that spread in all directions as far as the eye could see.

From the Florida everglades to the frozen wastes inhabited by the Eskimo, or Esquimaux, people; the vast land mass that makes up Canada and the United States of America covers geographical regions as diverse as the people who live in them. And their art, culture, food, music, and (of course) stitching traditions are just as many-splendoured – which makes this an excellent place to start our quilting world tour.

Trip around the world

THERE WAS ONLY ONE DESIGN I could do to begin this book, wasn't there? You'll probably have recognised it already: the traditional patchwork pattern known as Trip Around the World. Intriguingly the Amish people, who also use this design a great deal, call it Sunshine and Shadows – perhaps because travelling long distances isn't something that's part of the everyday Amish life. The design is created simply by piecing squares of the same size in a particular order – this is made extra-quick by using a variation on strip-piecing, so that you join strips of fabric first then chop them up to the required width. The pattern is often worked in bright, plain colours, but I've chosen to do it in shades of gold, orange and brown.

Finished size *65in (165cm) square*

Stitching guide The strip-piecing makes this an astonishingly quick way to piece a quilt of this size – a confident beginner could tackle it easily. Basic rotary cutting skills are useful. The instructions may make the design sound more complicated than it is; look at the diagrams and you'll soon see how the pattern comes together.

MATERIALS
- 10 different cotton fabrics, at least 40in (102cm) wide, 50cm of each
- Plain yellow backing fabric, 70in (180cm) square
- 2oz wadding or similar, 65in (165cm) square
- Yellow stitching thread
- Quilting threads to tone, or yellow buttonhole thread

INSTRUCTIONS

1 Press all the fabrics that will be used for the piecing, then cut four 4in (10cm) strips across the width of each fabric. (If you are doing this with a rotary cutter, you can layer several fabrics together and do them simultaneously.)

2 Lay the strips out in the order you want them to appear on the quilt (I've simply shaded mine from the lightest to the darkest). Using ¼in (5mm) seams, join each group of strips in that order. You now have four units as shown overleaf (**a**). Press all the seams to the darker side.

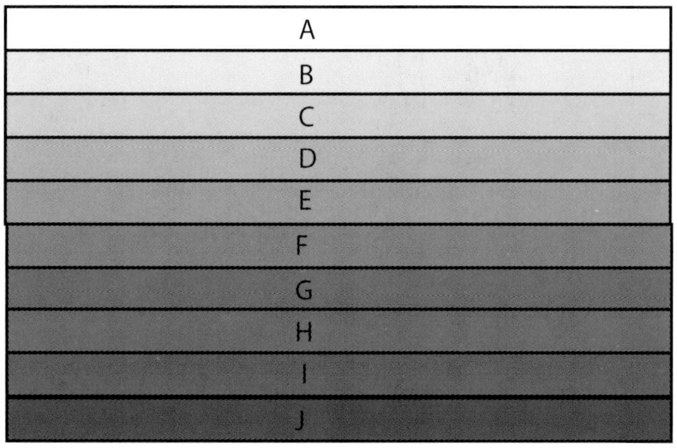

| A |
| B |
| C |
| D |
| E |
| F |
| G |
| H |
| I |
| J |

a

3 Lay these units carefully on top of each other, making sure that all the edges are aligned, and cut them, at right angles to the seams, into 4in (10cm) strips as shown (**b**). You now have 40 strips.

4 Take two strips and carefully unpick the square of fabric A from the end of one of them. (On my design this is the lightest square.) Set this aside. Join the rest of this strip to the first one so that square B on the second strip is joined to square A on the first one. Do exactly the same with two more short strips; you now have two long strips that look like this (**c**):

5 Take two more strips and unpick the squares of fabric J from each end (on my design, the darkest fabric). Take one of these squares and use it in the centre of your next long strip, making sure that the squares of fabric A are next to it. Do exactly the same with two more short strips. You now have two long strips that look like this (**d**):

6 Take two more strips and unpick the seams between fabrics H and I. Use one of these pairs of squares, and the spare square of J, and put them in the centre of the long strip as before. Do exactly the same with two more short strips. You now have two long strips that look like this (**e**):

7 Continue in the same way with all the remaining pairs of strips, taking off one more square from the end each time, to create a series of long strips as shown in the diagram (**f**). (Note, though, that you only have to do one version of the central strip, so you'll have two of the short strips left over.) Lay them out in order, to check that you've got the pattern right, then join the long strips in the correct order to create the quilt top. Press all the seams to one side.

8 Lay the large piece of yellow fabric on a flat surface, right side down, and position the wadding on top so that there's an even border of fabric all around. Lay the patchwork, right side up, on top of the wadding, then join the layers of the 'sandwich' using your chosen method (tacking, safety pinning etc). Quilt the design as you wish, by hand or machine; I just quilted it very simply using a wavy automatic stitch on my machine, stitching in yellow buttonhole thread down the central seam and then every third seam out to the edges.

9 Fold the edges of the yellow fabric to the front in a double fold to make an even border, then stitch in place by hand or machine.

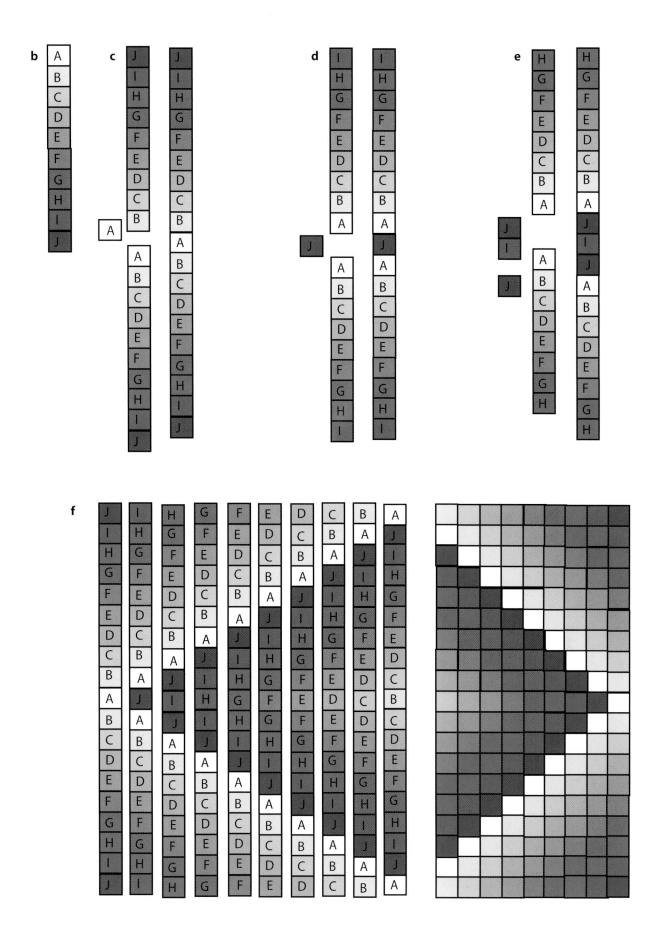

Fall wall-hanging

ONE OF MY AMBITIONS (shared by many people, I know) is to see Canada in the autumn – or fall, as it's evocatively called there. Even in photographs, the colours of the trees are breathtaking. For the project based on Canada I've taken the symbol of the country, the maple leaf, and built it into a wall-hanging in autumn colours to capture the spirit of the fall season. Each leaf is created separately, then the individual leaves are overlapped and stitched into an asymmetrical arrangement; the final hanging has a satisfying three-dimensional quality about it as the leaves create shadows on each other.

Finished size   *50x20in (127x50cm)*

Stitching guide   This project is easy and quick, even if you've never made appliqué motifs before. Almost all the stitching is done by machine. Save even more time by using part of a cheap tab-top curtain as the backing – that saves making the tabs separately. Use a mixture of plain and textured fabrics for your leaves, plus ones with tiny prints, to vary the look of the piece.

MATERIALS
- Heavy yellow ochre fabric, eg furnishing fabric, 42x19in (107x48cm), plus three 5x11in (13x28cm) strips for tabs
- Offcuts of cotton fabrics in autumn colours. For each leaf you'll need a piece 10x9in (25x23cm), and I've used 35 leaves – you can make each one different, or cut several from each fabric.
- Plain fabric in autumnal colours to back the leaves – one 10x9in (25x23cm) piece for each leaf
- Sewing thread in a toning colour
- Buttonhole thread in yellow
- Hanging rod with at least 17in (43cm) of hanging space
- Piece of thin card or template plastic, 10x9in (25x23cm)
- Pencil

INSTRUCTIONS

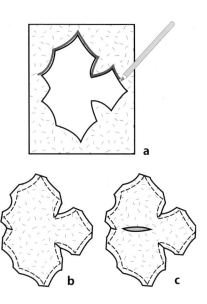

1 Stitch a half-inch (12mm) double hem round all edges of the heavy ochre fabric. Fold each spare strip of fabric in half along its length, right sides together, and stitch a half-inch (12mm) seam along the long edge. Turn out each tube and press flat with the seam at the centre back. Fold each tab in half, then position one tab at each of the top corners of the hanging and one in the centre; fold under the raw edges and secure the tabs by hand or machine stitching.

2 Trace or photocopy the solid outline of the leaf shape opposite, then stick it to thin card and cut it out (or trace the leaf onto the template plastic and cut it out). Use this as a template to trace the leaf shape onto the wrong side of each piece of leaf fabric (**a**).

3 Place each leaf fabric right sides together with a rectangle of backing fabric, and pin the two pieces together. Stitch by machine all the way round the marked leaf shapes. Trim each leaf shape to ½in (12mm) outside the stitched line, clipping across the outside corners and clipping into the inside corners (**b**).

4 Carefully, make a slit about 2in (5cm) long in the backing fabric at the centre top of each leaf (**c**); make sure that you don't cut the

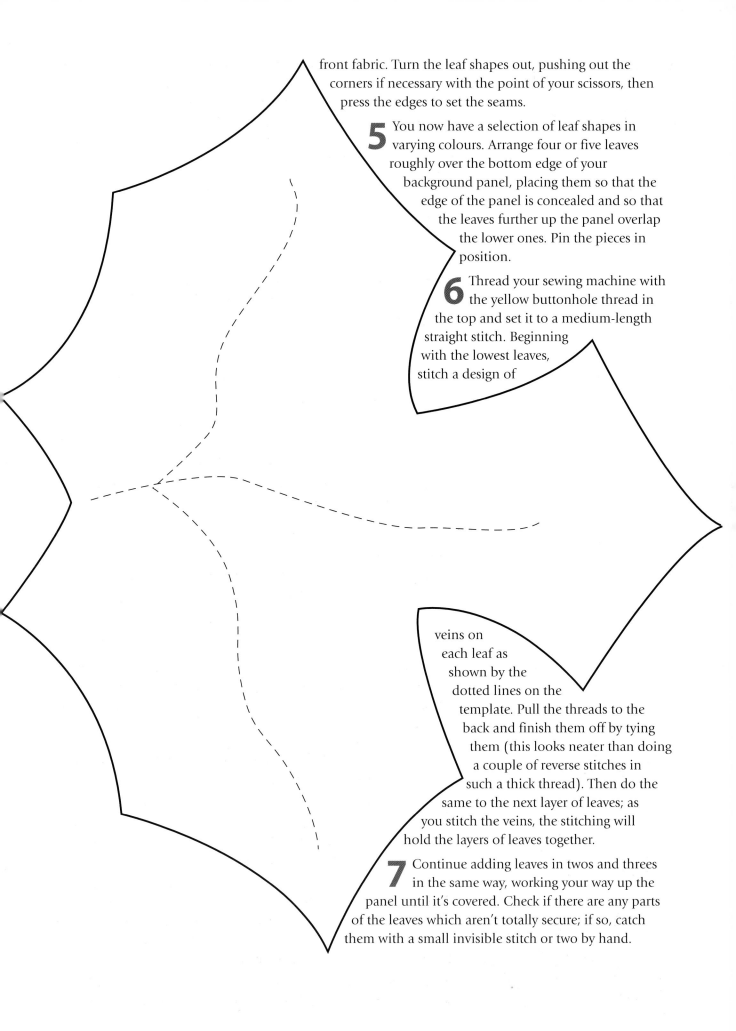

front fabric. Turn the leaf shapes out, pushing out the corners if necessary with the point of your scissors, then press the edges to set the seams.

5 You now have a selection of leaf shapes in varying colours. Arrange four or five leaves roughly over the bottom edge of your background panel, placing them so that the edge of the panel is concealed and so that the leaves further up the panel overlap the lower ones. Pin the pieces in position.

6 Thread your sewing machine with the yellow buttonhole thread in the top and set it to a medium-length straight stitch. Beginning with the lowest leaves, stitch a design of veins on each leaf as shown by the dotted lines on the template. Pull the threads to the back and finish them off by tying them (this looks neater than doing a couple of reverse stitches in such a thick thread). Then do the same to the next layer of leaves; as you stitch the veins, the stitching will hold the layers of leaves together.

7 Continue adding leaves in twos and threes in the same way, working your way up the panel until it's covered. Check if there are any parts of the leaves which aren't totally secure; if so, catch them with a small invisible stitch or two by hand.

Central & South America

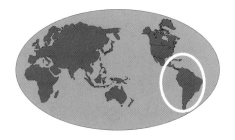

The closest I've been to Central or South America is a trip-of-a-lifetime to visit friends who were working in Trinidad; even there, the lush and colourful vegetation and the fantastic bird life gave me a tiny taste of some of the wonders of the mainland. Bright colours abounded; we found a giant samaan tree on the campus of the University of the West Indies, and would sit under it quietly; after a few minutes, the most beautiful birds I'd ever seen would come and settle in its branches – bright yellow saffron finches, tanagers in different shades, and several species of iridescent hummingbird. And the fabric shops were enough to make any quilter lose her reason ...

Central and South America abound in ancient civilisations – Inca, Aztec, Mayan etc – and many of their characteristic designs can still be seen in decorative wares and textiles today. I've tried to combine a bit of the old and bit of the new in the projects I've developed to celebrate this part of the world.

San Blas cat

JUST OFF THE EAST COAST of Panama lies a group of over 300 islands known as the San Blas Islands; about 50 of these are inhabited by the Cuna Indians, who have evolved the wonderful method of reverse appliqué known as San Blas appliqué or mola work. The work is done by layering several fabrics then cutting successive layers away in decorative designs to reveal the fabrics underneath; the raw edges are turned under and neatened with hand stitching. Many of the designs used by the Cuna are stylised animals and birds, and I've designed this cheeky cat wall-hanging in the Cuna tradition.

Finished size *26x34in (66x87cm)*

Stitching guide This project provides a good introduction to reverse appliqué for anyone who hasn't tried it before; the shapes are big and bold, and therefore not too fiddly to work with. Remember though that the appliqué is all done by hand, so if you don't like hand work it's not the method for you ...

MATERIALS
- One piece of blue cotton fabric 32x35in (81x89cm)
- One piece of red cotton fabric 26x34in (66x87cm)
- One piece of orange cotton fabric 26x34in (66x87cm)
- One piece of yellow cotton fabric 26x34in (66x87cm)
- One piece of green cotton fabric 6x3in (15x8cm)
- Sewing threads in blue, red and orange
- Stranded embroidery threads in yellow and blue
- Chalk marker
- Paper and pencil
- Black felt pen

INSTRUCTIONS

1 Enlarge the design on page 27 to the correct size. Use the grid method for this; on your paper, draw out a grid of 4in (10cm) squares, 8x6 squares. Transfer the lines within each grey square of the grid onto your drawing, enlarging them as you go. Go over the lines with black felt pen to make them clearer.

2 Lay the rectangle of blue fabric over the tracing so that the bottoms of the cat's feet are 6in (15cm) from the bottom edge of the fabric. Pin the two layers together so that they don't slip, then trace the lines marked 'blue' on the tracing onto the fabric, using the chalk marker. (If the fabric is too dark to see through easily, tape it onto a window on a sunny day, or use a lightbox if you have one.)

3 Lay the rectangle of red fabric on top of the rectangle of orange, so that their edges align, then lay the blue fabric on top of the two other pieces. Pin the layers together, then hold the whole design up to the light to double-check that the underneath fabrics cover the cat outline. When you're happy, tack the layers together an inch or so outside the cat outline (**a**).

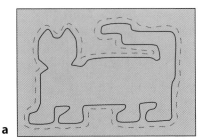

a

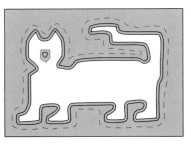

b

4 Using sharp-pointed embroidery scissors, carefully cut the blue fabric ¼in (5mm) inside the marked cat outline (**b**); make sure that you're only cutting the blue fabric, not the ones underneath. Clip any internal curves or corners.

c

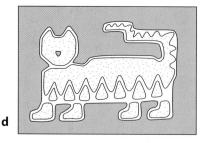

d

e

f

g

5 Thread a needle with blue thread and, beginning anywhere along the cat outline, start the first round of the appliqué. Turn the raw edges of the blue fabric under along the marked outline for an inch or two, then slipstitch the folded edge in place through the other layers; continue in the same way all round the outline, making smooth curves or sharp points as the pattern requires. Work all the way round the cat until all the raw edges of blue fabric have been secured.

6 Lay the appliqué over the design again and pin it into place; use the chalk marker to trace the lines marked 'red' onto the red fabric. To make sure that the red layer stays in position over the yellow layer, run a line of tacking along the centre of the zigzag section and another under the cat's chin (see diagram **c**).

7 In the same way as before, cut ¼in (5mm) inside the marked lines, then clip the edges, turn them under and slipstitch them in red. This time, you'll be working on several different sections to neaten the red edges and reveal the orange fabric underneath (**d**).

8 Once all the red edges are neatened, place the work over the drawn design again, pin, and use the chalk marker to draw in all the lines marked 'orange.' Unpin, then position the rectangle of yellow fabric behind the appliqué; hold it up to the light to check that all the marked lines are within the rectangle, then tack the layers together. Trim inside the marked lines as before (the only exception to this is the two lines round the eyes; leave them till the next stage); then clip, turn under and stitch the raw edges (**e**).

9 Pin the green fabric behind the eye area, making sure that the whole area is covered as before. Trim inside the eye lines as before, but this time making sure that you cut through both the orange and the yellow fabrics to reveal the green. Clip, turn under and stitch the two eye shapes in the usual way.

10 Using all six strands of the blue stranded cotton in a large sewing needle, embroider a pupil in each eye as shown (**f**) with an outline of backstitch and diagonal straight stitches. Using six strands of yellow, stitch backstitch whiskers under the nose and three curved claws on each foot as shown (**g**).

11 Fold each edge of the hanging under by ¼in (5mm) and then ½in (12mm); stitch the edge of each hem down by machine. Fold the top and bottom edges under by ½in (12mm) then 2in (5cm); machine the edges of the hem in place to produce casings. Hang the panel by putting poles through the top and bottom casings – or just the top, if you prefer.

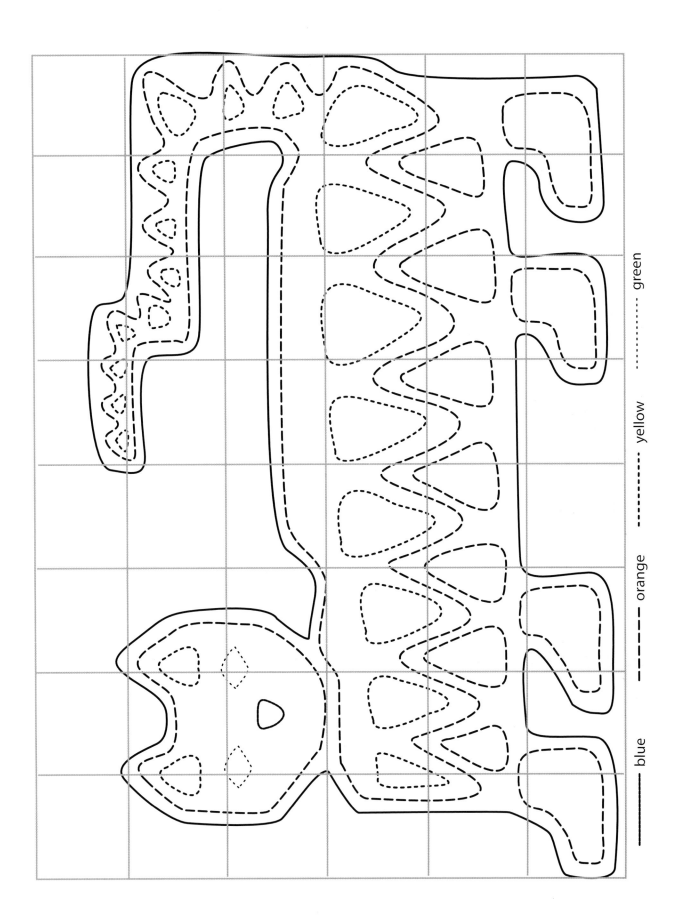

·········· green

------- yellow

------ orange

——— blue

Inca sun

STYLISED REPRESENTATIONS of the sun appear over and over again in the civilisations of South America, often reduced to a symbolic spiral with a few pointed rays coming out from it. I've gone for a half-way version; still recognisably a sun, but picking up the spiral motif in the centre. The bright colours convey the heat coming from the centre of the sun, and I found a sky-and-clouds fabric that set off the hot colours in just the right way. This would make a lovely wall-hanging for decorating a child's bedroom, or a centrepiece for a very dramatic double bed quilt.

Finished size   *42in (107cm) square*

Stitching guide   Another very quick project, as it uses 'rough-edge' appliqué – another way of putting 'not bothering to finish off the edges'! This technique seemed just right for the effect I wanted – looking like pieces of torn paper, quilted in a folk-art style with large running stitches in coloured coton à broder. If you're worried about the edges of the pieces fraying, you could back each of the sun pieces with lightweight iron-on interfacing before you roughen up the edges.

MATERIALS

- 42in (107cm) square of blue and white cotton 'sky' fabric
- 42in (107cm) square of 2oz polyester wadding or similar
- 46in (117cm) square of pale blue backing fabric
- 42x4in (107x10cm) strip of pale blue fabric for a casing
- Fat quarter of cotton fabric in mottled red
- ½yd (45cm) cotton fabric in mottled orange
- ½yd (45cm) cotton fabric in mottled bright yellow
- 40in (102cm) square of pale yellow cotton fabric
- Coton à broder, one skein each in yellow, orange, red and mid blue
- Pale blue sewing thread
- Chalk marker

INSTRUCTIONS

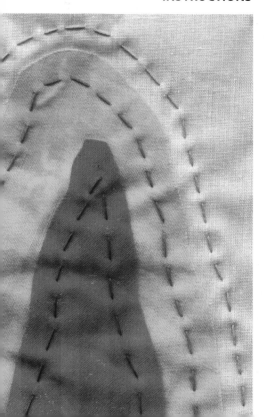

1 From the orange fabric, cut a circle 15in (39cm) in diameter. Now, using sharp scissors, cut round the edge of the circle deliberately roughly, moving the scissors randomly from side to side and snipping as you go. (To cut something out badly is quite hard to do first of all; if you're not sure about it, practise on some fabric offcuts first. You'll soon get the hang of it.) This creates the 'torn paper' effect. If any bits of the edge still look too neat, have another go at them with the scissors.

2 From the red fabric, also cut a circle 15in (39cm) in diameter. On this circle, use the chalk marker to draw a rough, thick spiral (see diagram **a**). Now, use the 'torn paper' cutting technique to cut round the edges of the spiral.

a

3 Trace or photocopy the sun ray templates on page 30. Use the larger one (**A**) to cut seven pieces from the bright yellow fabric, and the smaller one (**B**) to cut seven pieces from the remaining orange fabric; now use the 'torn paper' technique on all these pieces.

4 Press the pale yellow fabric and lay the orange circle in the centre. Arrange the yellow rays evenly around the edge of the circle,

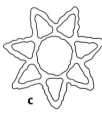

b

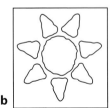

c

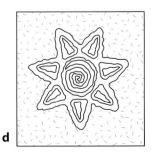

d

leaving a gap of about an inch (2.5cm) between the rays and the edge of the circle (**b**). Pin the rays in place, then use the same 'torn paper' technique to cut the pale yellow fabric into a rough sun shape as shown (**c**), leaving a margin of about 2in (5cm) round the edges of the rays.

5 Lay the wadding out on a flat surface and smooth out any creases. Press the background 'sky' fabric and lay it out on top of the wadding, right side up, then lay the pale yellow sun shape in the centre and pin it in position. Pin the spiral inside the circle, then arrange the orange ray pieces (at this stage these look disconcertingly like carrots!) at one side of each yellow ray as shown (**d**) and pin in position.

6 Using orange coton à broder, quilt around the edges of the spiral using large running stitches; make the stitches about twice as large on the front of the work as on the back (like sashiko stitching – see

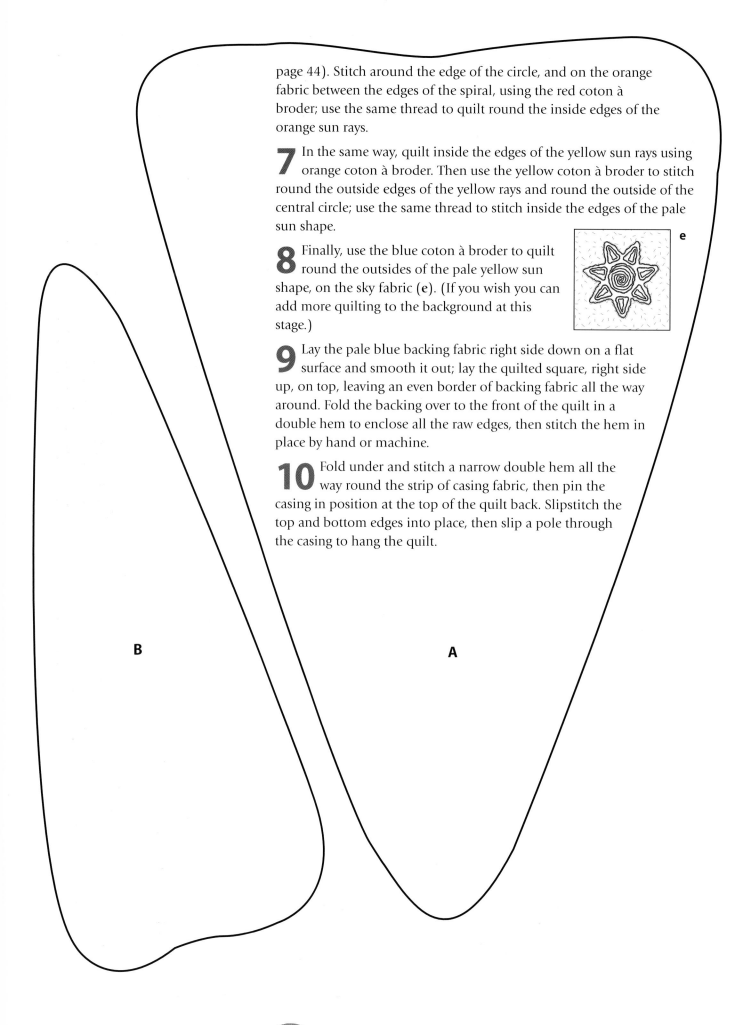

page 44). Stitch around the edge of the circle, and on the orange fabric between the edges of the spiral, using the red coton à broder; use the same thread to quilt round the inside edges of the orange sun rays.

7 In the same way, quilt inside the edges of the yellow sun rays using orange coton à broder. Then use the yellow coton à broder to stitch round the outside edges of the yellow rays and round the outside of the central circle; use the same thread to stitch inside the edges of the pale sun shape.

8 Finally, use the blue coton à broder to quilt round the outsides of the pale yellow sun shape, on the sky fabric (**e**). (If you wish you can add more quilting to the background at this stage.)

e

9 Lay the pale blue backing fabric right side down on a flat surface and smooth it out; lay the quilted square, right side up, on top, leaving an even border of backing fabric all the way around. Fold the backing over to the front of the quilt in a double hem to enclose all the raw edges, then stitch the hem in place by hand or machine.

10 Fold under and stitch a narrow double hem all the way round the strip of casing fabric, then pin the casing in position at the top of the quilt back. Slipstitch the top and bottom edges into place, then slip a pole through the casing to hang the quilt.

B

A

Although Australia and New Zealand are a thousand miles apart, they're often considered together in people's minds because they're both English-speaking, and both so far away from most other places! I'd be intrigued to see Australia, although the large number of eight-legged beasties is a little offputting for an arachnophobe; apparently New Zealand has only one poisonous spider (by this I assume they mean one species rather than one individual ...), so maybe that would be a better bet.

Both Australia and New Zealand have the cultures of their indigenous peoples mingled with many elements of modern western society, which must create intriguing mixes; there is also spectacular quilting going on in both countries, with quilters developing individual styles based on their own heritage and their local fauna and flora.

Lizard footstool

IN RECENT YEARS there's been a great interest in the art of the Australian Aboriginal people. A while ago I bought a book featuring lots of examples of Aboriginal art, and was captivated by the colours and textures; the earth colours and impure greens and ochres are very different from the palette I usually gravitate towards, and I decided to use them in a large quilt called *Treefrog Dreaming*. I did lots of sketches and drawings of typical Aboriginal designs and incorporated some of them into the border of the quilt; this friendly lizard was developed from one of those drawings.

Finished size *to fit a footstool pad 16x12in (41x30cm)*

Stitching guide This project is about as quick and simple as you could hope for, especially if you're already adept with machine appliqué using satin stitch. Choose fabrics that have a slightly ethnic feel about their colours and textures to give the design the right kind of effect.

MATERIALS
- One piece of dark mottled cotton fabric for the background 20x16in (51x41cm)
- One piece of mottled cream cotton fabric for the lizard body 15x10in (38x25cm)
- One piece of mottled brown cotton fabric for the body pattern 6x4in (15x10cm)
- Bondaweb or Heat 'n' Bond 15x10in (38x25cm)
- Machine embroidery thread in beige
- Pencil
- Piece of Stitch 'n' Tear or cartridge paper 15x10in (38x25cm)

INSTRUCTIONS

1 Use a photocopier to enlarge the templates on page 35 by 140%, or use the grid method (see page 41). Trace the lizard shape (**A**) onto the paper side of the bonding web, and cut the shape out roughly.

2 Lay the bonding web, web (rough) side down, on the wrong side of the lizard body fabric and fuse it into place. Cut the shape out neatly along the marked lines.

3 Trace pieces **B** and **C** onto the remaining bonding web; cut these out roughly and fuse them onto the back of the body pattern fabric, then cut the pieces out neatly as before.

4 Lay the body piece, right side up, on the background fabric so that there's an even border of fabric all round the lizard shape. When you're happy with the positioning, fuse the shape into place on the background. Lay the large diamond-shaped piece of fabric onto the lizard's body and the smaller one on his head; fuse them into position.

5 Thread your sewing machine with the machine embroidery thread and set it to a medium-width satin stitch (about 2/2.5mm width). Pin the Stitch 'n' Tear or cartridge paper behind the design, then go round all the edges of the fused pieces with satin stitch. Tear the foundation paper away from the back of the design.

6 Follow the manufacturer's instructions to mount the background fabric on the footstool pad and assemble the footstool. (For the stool in the photograph I stretched the fabric over the pad and held it in place with squirts from a hot glue gun; the pad then had to be secured in the frame with two screws.)

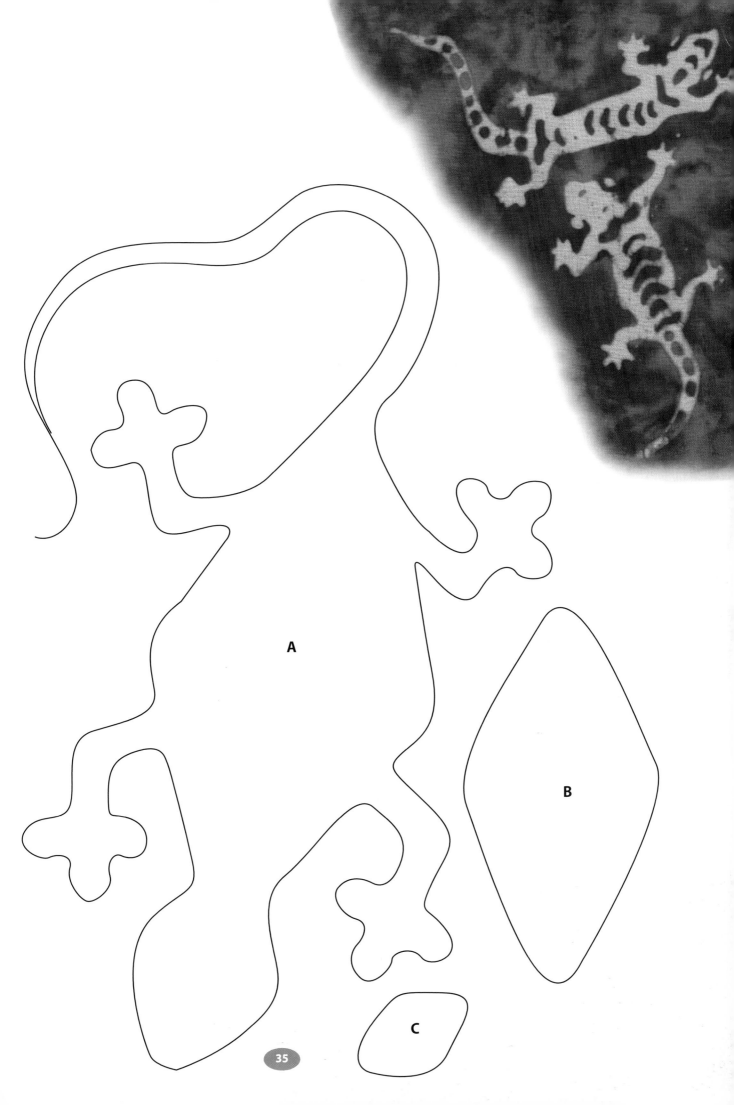

A

B

C

The Orient

We're so familiar with Chinese and Japanese art and crafts nowadays that it's hard to believe they were virtually unknown to the western world 150 years ago. But once the west began to glimpse oriental art and design, it was love at first sight – eastern influences immediately appeared in everything from the music of Gilbert and Sullivan and the furniture in the smart shops to the paintings of the Impressionists. And the art of the east is just as appealing to today's eye; it still conjures up something that's unusual, exotic, mysterious – and the spare beauty of the lines delights quilters and other artists.

I've interpreted two very different traditional oriental motifs for this section, stitching them in totally different ways to show just how versatile they can be for the modern quilter.

Mandarin ducks

FOR SEVERAL YEARS I've been wanting to create a quilt based on the lovely shapes of mandarin ducks, and this book gave me the perfect opportunity. Two mandarin ducks are often used as a symbol of marital harmony in Chinese art – a bit like having two doves or lovebirds in western art. I've stitched this quilt in stained glass patchwork, which is a very quick way of producing a quilt this size because you don't have to do any seaming or piecing, or any complicated appliqué. I wanted to give the design a slightly folk-art feel, so I've deliberately created large patches in the foliage and the border so that I could embellish them with large, bold stitching and coloured wooden buttons.

Finished size

83x60in (212x152cm)

Stitching guide

Although this is a full-size quilt, the stained glass patchwork method makes it very quick and easy to create. As you stitch the bias binding on (by hand or machine, but machine is much quicker), you're quilting the piece at the same time. Once the basic design is completed, you can add as much or as little hand embellishment as you want. I've used fabrics with small patterns or mottled textures to add visual interest to the large areas.

MATERIALS

- One piece of mottled blue 'water' fabric 65x43in (165x110cm)
- One piece of black backing fabric 87x64in (222x162cm)
- 2oz polyester wadding or similar 83x60in (212x152cm)
- Thin white cotton sheeting or firm muslin 83x60in (212x152cm)
- 2yd (2m) brightly-patterned cotton fabric for the border and the spiral branch
- 1yd (1m) purple fabric for the border
- Yellow ochre fabric for the internal border, at least 76x56in (193x143cm) (to save fabric on this section you can piece the yellow ochre border from 6in (15cm) wide strips – you'll need about 7yd (7m) of strips in total)
- ³⁄₄yd (70cm) dark green fabric
- ¹⁄₂yd (45cm) mid green fabric
- ¹⁄₂yd (45cm) brown batik fabric for the pointed leaves
- Fat quarters of light green for the plants, mottled pale yellow for the female duck's body, rust-red print for the insides of the large leaves, and two dark blue small-print fabrics for the birds' main wings
- Large scraps of other cotton fabrics in shades of purple, orange, gold, jade, rust, yellow and turquoise for the flowers and all the small feathers
- Two shiny black buttons, approx ¹⁄₂in (12mm) wide, for the eyes
- 6yd (6m) blue bias binding, ¹⁄₂in (12mm) when folded
- 50yd (50m) black bias binding, ¹⁄₂in (12mm) when folded
- Two reels of black rayon machine embroidery thread
- Blue and black sewing thread
- Pack of dressmakers' tracing paper

- Clear tape
- Pencil and black felt pen
- Stitch 'n' Tear or cartridge paper

Optional extras for embellishment:

- *Plain or space-dyed coton à broder, one skein each in turquoise and green, and two skeins in mixed bright colours*
- *About 150 flat, round wooden buttons in assorted sizes and colours*

INSTRUCTIONS

1 Stick several sheets of tracing paper together until you have a piece that is at least 90x60in (130x152cm). Draw a grid of 10in (25cm) squares – nine squares up by six squares across – onto the paper in pencil.

2 The master drawing for the quilt is on page 43. You'll see that the design has a grey grid over it; this grid matches the one that you've drawn onto your tracing paper. Copy the solid lines of the design onto your own grid, enlarging them as you go, until you have a full-size design. Go over the lines with black felt pen to make them stronger.

3 Press the piece of white sheeting or muslin and lay it over the design; trace the lines onto the fabric in pencil (don't worry about the marks, or about making mistakes; everything is going to be covered up by fabric or bias binding).

4 Mark the different sections of the design with the words and numbers shown on the original; this ensures that you know which piece is which once you've started cutting the pattern up. Cut up the tracing along the solid lines, and put the pieces that go together in separate batches (eg, put all the purple border pieces together so that they're all ready when you come to cut up that fabric). (If you think you may want to do this design again, trace the pattern pieces individually onto new pieces of tracing paper and cut them up, so that you leave your original design in one piece.)

5 Use the cut pieces as templates to cut shapes from the appropriate fabrics, cutting just outside the lines to give extra margin for error! Most of the pieces are asymmetric, so make sure that you always put the template right side up on the right side of the fabric. Don't feel you have to follow my colour layout for the birds slavishly; mix the colours around so that there's a good contrast among all the different feathers. As you cut each piece, pin it in position on the white fabric.

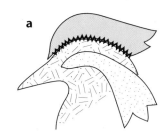

a

6 Once all the pieces have been cut and positioned, you may find it helpful just to run a line of zigzag stitching in black along all the joins between patches (**a**). This helps to stop them from wriggling while you do the next stages; it's a lot quicker and surer than tacking, and you don't have to take the stitches out later – they'll be covered by the bias binding.

7 Set your machine to the widest satin stitch it will do, and thread it with the black machine embroidery thread. Position a piece of Stitch 'n' Tear or cartridge paper under the relevant area, and stitch a line of satin stitch along each of the lines indicated by a dotted line on the master drawing. As you complete each line, pull the foundation paper away from the back of the design.

b

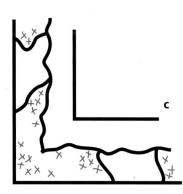

c

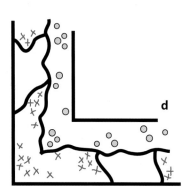

d

8 Press the black backing fabric and lay it, right side down, on a flat surface, smoothing out any wrinkles. Lay the wadding on top so that there's an even border of fabric all the way around. Place the quilt top on top of the wadding, right side up; secure the layers together using your favourite method (eg tacking, tack-gun, safety pins etc).

9 Follow the dashed lines on the master drawing to see where the lines of blue bias binding go. Pin these into position, folding under the tips to make long points where they finish in the water. Where the end of a line meets a new patch of fabric, just leave this end raw; it will be covered by the black bias binding when the design is outlined. Stitch down each side of the blue binding lines using a small machine zigzag in blue.

10 Now you need to begin building up the stained glass effect. Follow the guidelines below to build up the design, working basically from the centre of the design outwards. As you stitch the edges of each line of bias binding, you're quilting the design at the same time.

11 Once all the black bias binding is stitched in position, fold the edges of the backing over in a double hem to the front of the quilt and stitch the fold in place by machine. Add the black buttons to the ducks to create eyes. Your quilt is now complete; if you wish you can follow the next step to embellish it, or you can leave it as it is!

12 Use turquoise coton à broder to work random wavy lines of large running stitches across the blue background fabric to suggest ripples of water. Use the green thread to stitch large random straight stitches at different angles across the pale green and mid green sections of the foliage; this technique is known as seeding (**b**). Use the bright-coloured threads to stitch random cross stitches onto parts of the purple border sections (**c**). Scatter the buttons randomly around the yellow border, and hold each button in place with several straight stitches in the bright threads (**d**).

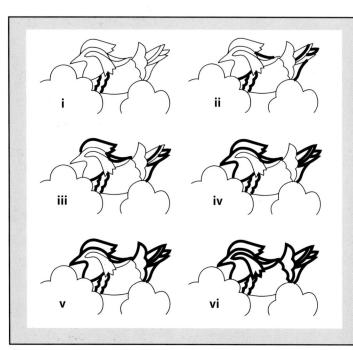

i   ii   iii   iv   v   vi

Note on building up stained glass patchwork designs

Always stitch first any lines that tuck in under other lines – so, for instance, on the male duck, the first bits to be stitched are the two scalloped lines across the body front, as the raw ends of these lines will be covered by later pieces of binding.

You can see in the sequence on the left how the other lines of that duck are then built up. Follow this way of doing things throughout the design; as you come to each part, stop and think which lines have their ends covered by other lines. And if you make a mistake, don't worry – just undo a few stitches, tuck the raw end of the bias binding underneath, and re-stitch over the top!

patterned 1

purple 1

patterned 2

purple 2

yellow ochre

rust red

blue

blue

blue

rust red

brown

patterned 3

blue

blue

brown

rust red

patterned

purple 7

blue

blue

patterned 7

pale yellow

dark green

dark blue

mid green

light green

purple 6

blue

blue

purple 3

dark green

dark blue

dark green

patterned 6

mid green

blue

mid green

light green

blue

purple 5

patterned 5

purple 4

patterned 4

.... black satin stitch

- - - - blue bias binding

Sashiko firescreen

JAPAN, OF COURSE, has its own rich heritage of quilting; Japanese stitchers have given the quilting world the technique known as sashiko, which is like a cross between quilting and embroidery. It's worked in running stitches, just like ordinary quilting, but the stitches are meant to show; they're larger – usually twice as long on the front of the work as they are on the back – and are worked in thicker thread. The traditional colours for sashiko work are white thread on an indigo blue background, but it looks wonderful in other colours too. I like working this kind of quilting on silk, and I've used a mid-green silk for this bamboo design, backed by a typical sashiko repeat pattern. You can buy special white sashiko thread, but coton à broder is often easier to find and works just as well.

Finished size *to fit a firescreen measuring 15½x19½in (40x50cm) within the frame*

Stitching guide A quick and easy design; if you're new to sashiko this will be an ideal first project, and if you're already familiar with the technique you'll have it finished in no time. If the dimensions of your firescreen are slightly different, draw a rectangle the size of your inside frame, mark lines 1in (2.5cm) in from each edge, then draw the bamboo design in the centre; add extra repeats of the background pattern as needed to fill out the space.

MATERIALS
- One piece of mid-green silk dupion 18x22in (46x56cm)
- One piece of firm, flat wadding 15½x19½in (40x50cm)
- Two skeins of white coton à broder
- White pencil crayon
- Paper, pencil and black felt pen if you're drawing the design rather than photocopying
- Firescreen with a dark green frame

INSTRUCTIONS

1 Enlarge the design on page opposite to the correct size (175% on a photocopier, or use the grid method described on page 41). If you've drawn up the design, go over the lines in black felt pen to make them stronger.

2 Press the green silk and lay it over the design, right side up, so that there's an even border of fabric all the way around the design; pin the two layers together. Trace all the lines using the white pencil crayon; keep it sharp so that it makes strong lines. If you find it difficult to see the design through the silk, tape the paper and fabric to a window on a sunny day, or use a lightbox. Unpin.

3 Lay the wadding down on a flat surface and smooth it out, then position the marked design, right side up, on top of the wadding so that there's an even border of wadding all round the edges of the design (you can check this by holding it up to the light, or by smoothing the silk down to reveal the shape of the padded rectangle underneath). Tack the layers together with a few lines of stitching horizontally and vertically.

4 Thread a large, sharp sewing needle with the white coton à broder and, beginning in the centre of the design, work large, even

sashiko stitches around the bamboo design. Next, work the outline all round the bamboo shape, then stitch the background pattern, and finally the two borders; make sure you keep the border lines nice and straight, and at an even distance from each other. Remove the tacking threads.

5 Follow the manufacturer's instructions to assemble the firescreen. For the one in the photograph, this simply meant stretching the design across the central board and taping it in place on the back, then securing the board in the frame with the integral clips.

India

India is another place on my 'maybe one day' list, but I've been intrigued to read some of the things that quilter Gisela Thwaites has written about it. She has fallen in love with the country, and it's been the main influence on her exotic crazy patchwork pieces, embellished using many of the specialised techniques that she's been taught in Indian villages.

Glitz is one of the things we associate with Indian textiles – gilt threads used for embroidery and woven into brocade fabrics; the sheen of silk fabrics; shiny beads and sequins incorporated into the embroidery or made into fringes; and of course the glints of shisha mirrors among all the other rich colours and textures. And it's not just in textiles that we see the richness of Indian design; tiles, metalwork, woodcarving – lush patterns are everywhere. Even the way in which spices are laid out in the market provides a feast for the eyes as well as the nose! I've tried to capture some of that richness in the project and the pattern library for this section.

Crazy patchwork boxes

CRAZY PATCHWORK can be built up in many different ways, and I think I've found the easiest way of all! These box tops use a combination of crazy patchwork and stained glass patchwork; the patches don't have to be neatened, because the lines of braid cover the raw edges, and by using different braids it increases the crazy effect. I've used exotic and glitzy fabrics and braids, but you could do these designs just as easily using cottons – they'd look great done in Christmassy fabrics on green, red, blue or gold boxes, with Christmas ribbons and braids used as the 'leading.'

Finished size   *You can adapt this design to fit any square or rectangular box*

Stitching guide   A fantastically quick way of getting spectacular results; the stitching is quickest on the machine, but you could stitch the braids on by hand if you prefer. You can also embellish the braids and the fabric patches with hand embroidery and beads for extra sparkle.

MATERIALS

- One piece of white foundation fabric, 1in (2.5cm) larger all round than your box lid
- One piece of 2oz polyester wadding the same size as your box lid
- One piece of thick card the same size as your box lid
- Pencil and paper
- Large scraps of glitzy fabrics and braids in colours to tone with your box
- Strong glue
- Sewing thread to tone with your colourscheme

INSTRUCTIONS

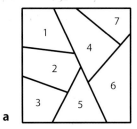

a

1 Lay your box lid face down on the paper and trace round it in pencil. Use a ruler and pencil to divide the tracing into random patches; begin by drawing a diagonal line randomly across the whole area, then draw other lines at different angles (**a**). The larger your box lid, the more patches you can include – don't make them too small, as you'll be using quite thick braid round each patch. Add a line one inch (2.5cm) outside each edge of the drawn square (**b**).

2 Lay your white foundation fabric over the drawing and trace the lines onto the fabric in pencil (**c**).

3 Decide which fabric is going where, then cut up the tracing and use the

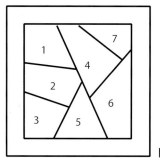

b

c

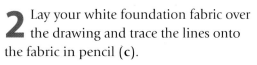

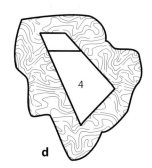

pieces as templates to cut the fabrics. Remember to use the templates right side up on the right side of the fabric (d). As you cut each piece, pin it in place on the foundation square. (Some smooth metallic fabrics mark if you put a pin through them – if in doubt, pin right at the edge where the marks will be covered by braid.)

4 Cut pieces of braid to cover each line of the design (you don't need to add braid round the outside edges as these will be hidden). Begin with the lines whose ends will be covered by other pieces of braid (see **e**), and stitch the pieces of braid in place by hand or machine so that they cover the raw edges of the patches (**f**). The final line will be the line that goes all the way across the design (**g**).

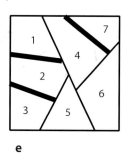

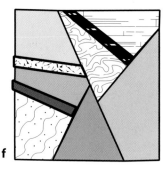
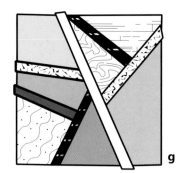

5 Press the design gently from the back, making sure that the iron isn't too hot so that it doesn't melt any of the metallic fabrics or braids.

6 Spread a little glue across the cardboard shape and stick the wadding in place. Leave to dry completely.

7 Lay the patchwork piece face down on a flat surface and position the cardboard shape, wadding side down, on top. Fold the corners of the foundation square over to the back and glue them in place (h), then glue the edges down firmly (i).

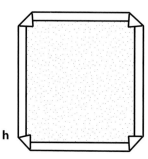
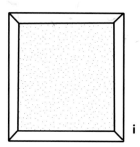

8 Spread glue generously over the wrong side of the card shape, making sure you go right to the edges, and leave until just tacky. Press the card onto the top of the box lid, and put a heavy weight on top until the glue is completely dry (don't worry about squashing the wadding; it'll spring back into shape as soon as you remove the weight).

The Middle East

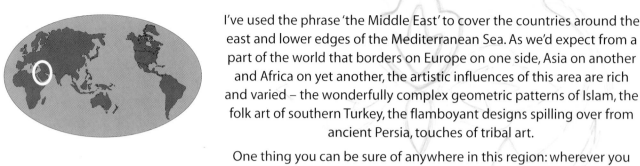

I've used the phrase 'the Middle East' to cover the countries around the east and lower edges of the Mediterranean Sea. As we'd expect from a part of the world that borders on Europe on one side, Asia on another and Africa on yet another, the artistic influences of this area are rich and varied – the wonderfully complex geometric patterns of Islam, the folk art of southern Turkey, the flamboyant designs spilling over from ancient Persia, touches of tribal art.

One thing you can be sure of anywhere in this region: wherever you go, you'll see beautiful patterns. A trip to Israel furnished me with enough inspiration to last a lifetime: the decorative designs on Jerusalem's Dome of the Rock alone would keep any quilter busy for a long time. Not that I intend to stop travelling and looking for more inspiration, you understand ...

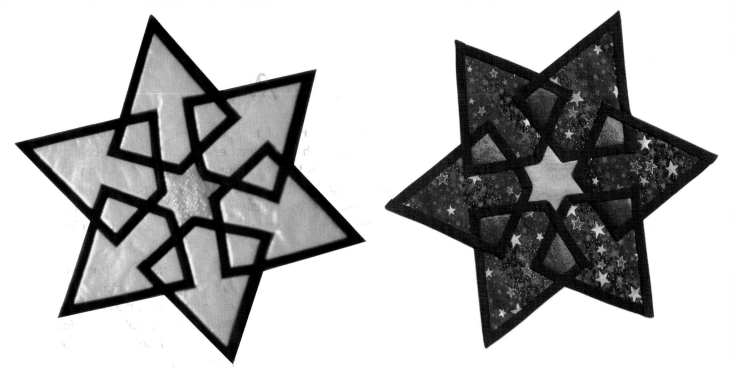

Christmas star

THE INTERWEAVING DESIGNS of Islamic patterns often have star shapes at the centre. When the theme of the the Quilts UK show at Malvern was Stars a few years ago, I chose a complex Islamic pattern to make a quilt called *Stained Glass Star*. So many people have expressed interest in it that I thought I'd create a small Christmas star for this book. The design is created from six identical interlocking shapes; if you use a firm, compact wadding, the star is firm enough to hang flat against a wall without the tips drooping – I used Needle Punch.

Finished size   *16in (41cm) diameter*

Stitching guide   The design is straightforward to do and very quick to stitch; it uses basic stained glass patchwork, but because there are no curves you can use black tape or ribbon for the 'leading' instead of bias binding. To make the opalescent star, I just drew the design out in full on the opalescent fabric (without cutting out separate sections), then added the star shape in the centre before stitching on the tape.

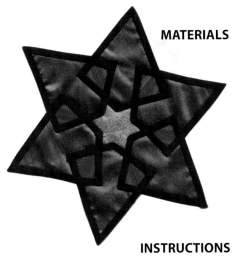

MATERIALS

- Metallic blue fabric 16in (41cm) square
- Large scraps of gold and red metallic fabrics
- One 16in (41cm) square of firm, flat wadding
- One 16in (41cm) square of white foundation fabric
- Black sewing thread
- 5yd (5m) black ribbon or tape, ½in (12mm) wide
- One small curtain rings
- Thin card, or template plastic

INSTRUCTIONS

1 Trace or photocopy the three shapes on page 54; stick them onto the card and cut them out. (If you're using template plastic, simply trace the shapes and cut them out.) Use the large arrow-shaped template (**A**) to cut out six shapes from the blue metallic fabric, the diamond-shaped template (**B**) to cut six shapes from the red, and the star-shaped template (**C**) to cut one shape from the gold fabric.

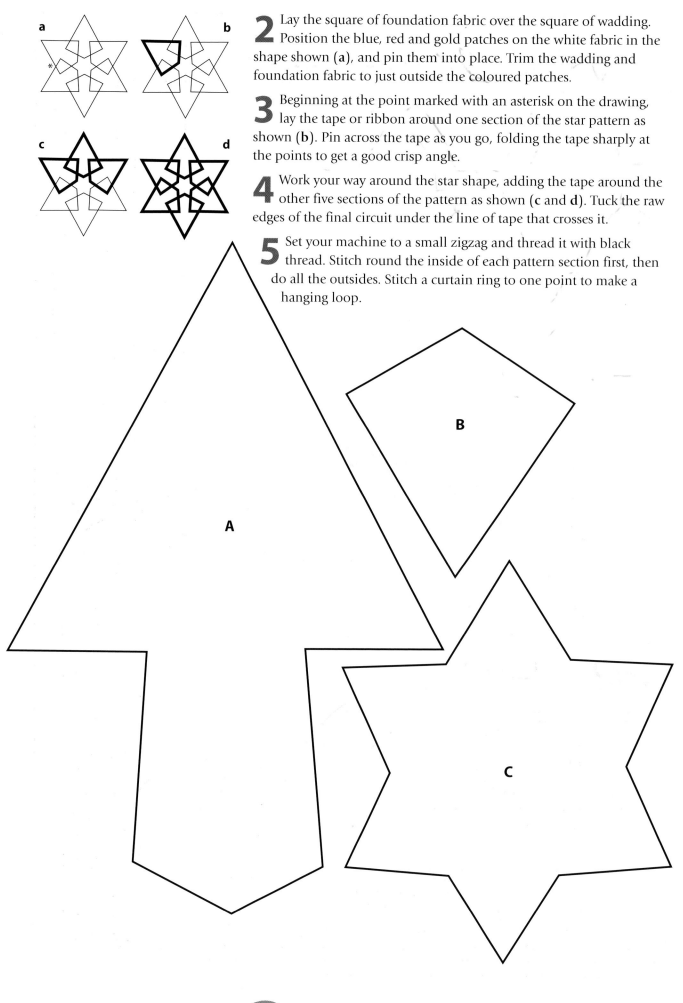

2 Lay the square of foundation fabric over the square of wadding. Position the blue, red and gold patches on the white fabric in the shape shown (**a**), and pin them into place. Trim the wadding and foundation fabric to just outside the coloured patches.

3 Beginning at the point marked with an asterisk on the drawing, lay the tape or ribbon around one section of the star pattern as shown (**b**). Pin across the tape as you go, folding the tape sharply at the points to get a good crisp angle.

4 Work your way around the star shape, adding the tape around the other five sections of the pattern as shown (**c** and **d**). Tuck the raw edges of the final circuit under the line of tape that crosses it.

5 Set your machine to a small zigzag and thread it with black thread. Stitch round the inside of each pattern section first, then do all the outsides. Stitch a curtain ring to one point to make a hanging loop.

a

b

c

d

A

B

C

Central Europe

As well as the massive country of Russia, Central Europe includes many countries which are just emerging from Soviet influence and taking great delight in re-establishing their own national identities. Folk art flourishes in different ways in the traditional art of all the countries of this region, and is seen in woodcarving, painting and metalwork as well as in household textiles and national costumes.

Designs of this type are often built up using bright colours and simple shapes, stylised so that they can be reproduced quickly and easily. The designs are frequently based on natural forms such as flowers, fruit, trees and birds; hearts are a favourite motif too. I've chosen two of these favourite folk-art themes, fruit and hearts, for the projects to represent this part of the world.

Fruit cushion

THIS FOLK-ART DESIGN gives the impression of being stencilled, but it's actually worked in the technique known as shadow quilting, or shadow appliqué. Shapes are cut from bright fabric, then laid on a white background and covered with a layer of sheer fabric (in this case, muslin, though you can use tulle, organza or lace). The sheer fabric softens the colours, and the pieces are then held in place by stitching round the edge of each shape – these lines of stitching also quilt the project at the same time. I've made the square block up into a cushion-cover, but of course you could do several and build them into a large quilt if you're feeling ambitious!

Finished size   *17in (42.5cm) square*

Stitching guide   Even if you've never done shadow-work before, you'll find this project very straightforward; there are no tricky techniques. The stitching is all done by hand – it's one of those rare techniques where it's actually less fiddly to stitch by hand than by machine. Prepare the design during the day, then sit and do the restful hand-quilting over an evening or two in front of the television.

MATERIALS
- One 18in (45cm) square of white cotton fabric
- Two 18x12in (45x30cm) rectangles of white cotton fabric for the cushion backs
- Two 18in (45cm) squares of white muslin
- One 18in (45cm) square of 2oz polyester wadding
- 16in (41cm) square of thin Bondaweb or Heat 'n' Bond (you'll probably need to buy this off the roll; the packs of Bondaweb sold ready-cut are about 18in wide, but not long enough)
- Large scraps of bright fabric (the type of fabric doesn't matter: cotton, silk, satin etc) in these colours:
  orange; purple; red; plum (eg purply-red); peach; three or four different types of green (eg yellowy green, dark green, leaf green); yellow ochre (not a pale yellow, or it will disappear!)
- Ordinary sewing threads, or quilting threads, in the same range of colours
- Pencil and rubber
- Pencil crayon in a pale colour
- Paper scissors
- One 18in (45cm) square cushion pad

1 Photocopy the two designs on pages 58 and 59, enlarging them to 15in (38cm) square. (The designs are mirror images; this is because the shapes of the bonding web are reversed as you fuse them.)

2 Lay your bonding web, paper side up, over the pattern with the writing on, and trace all the lines in pencil. Mark in all the names as shown on the tracing; this will help you when you come to fuse the shapes onto the different fabrics. Cut roughly round all the shapes, leaving a small margin outside the marked lines; when several pieces appear side by side, eg the pineapple, or the bunch of grapes, leave them as one piece; don't cut each bit out individually.

peach

orange leaf

orange

leaf

cherry

leaf

vine leaf

vine leaf

leaf

leaf

leaf

orange

grape 1

cherry

grape 4

grape 2   grape 3

pineapple top

cherry

grape 5   grape 6   grape 7   grape 8

orange

2   pineapple 4

pineapple 7

pineapple 1   pineapple 5   pineapple 8   11

grape 5   grape 6   grape 7   grape 8

9   grape 10   grape 11   grape 12

3   12

13

apple leaf

plum leaf   pineapple 6   pineapple 9

strawberry leaf

10

apple

plum   plum

pear

strawberry

strawberry

strawberry leaf   strawberry

a

b

c

d

e

3 Lay your square of white fabric over the other fruit drawing (the one without the writing) so that there's an even border of fabric all the way around; pin the two together to stop them wriggling. Use a pale crayon to trace round all the lines of the drawing; this will help you to position all the pieces when you've cut them out.

4 Choose which coloured fabric you will use for the different fruits and leaves; when you've chosen, fuse the matching piece(s) of bonding web onto the back of the fabric (**a**). (The rough side of the bonding web always goes on the wrong side of the fabric.) Cut each piece out round the marked lines (**b**).

5 Peel the backing paper off the bonding web pieces (**c**) and lay them in position on your marked square of white fabric (**d**). When you are happy with the arrangement, fuse all the pieces in position with a warm iron (**e**).

6 Lay one of the muslin squares on a flat surface and position the wadding on top. Lay the decorated square, right side up, on top of the wadding. Lay the second muslin square over the top of the fruit design (**f**). Tack the layers together with a few lines of tacking stitch in each direction.

7 Use the appropriate-coloured threads to quilt round the edges of each piece of fruit, using fairly small running stitches (**g**). When all the quilting is complete, remove the tacking threads.

8 To make the panel up into a cushion, press and stitch a small double hem along one long edge of each rectangle of white fabric. Lay the fruit square, right side up, on a flat surface and position the rectangles, right side down, so that they overlap and the raw edges match those of the square. Stitch a half-inch seam round all four edges. Clip the corners and turn the cushion-cover out, then press the seams at just the very edge of the cushion-cover to set them.

Hearts photograph album

THAT OTHER GREAT MAINSTAY of folk art, the heart, is the focus of this design. I've managed to find lots of different fabrics printed with heart designs in shades of red, white, blue and gold, but the design would look just as effective worked in a different colourway. You could work the design in shades of cream, with a gold or silver binding, as a really special wedding present for a lucky couple – or pick out appropriate colours to celebrate a silver, gold, ruby or emerald wedding anniversary.

Finished size *To fit a photograph album front at least 10½x13in (27x33cm)*

Stitching guide This design is another variation on stained glass patchwork, using the fusible narrow bias binding that's become very popular with quilters. This binding has a little strip of bonding web on the back, which holds it in place while you're stitching. The project is quick and straightforward to stitch.

MATERIALS

- One piece of heavy interfacing 10½x13in (27x33cm)
- One piece of bonding web 10½x13in (27x33cm)
- Large scraps of cotton fabrics in toning heart prints (or use a mixture of folk prints and plain fabrics)
- 4yd (4m) fusible bias binding, ¼in (5mm) wide, in navy blue (or a colour to tone with your fabrics)
- Stitching thread to match your bias binding
- Pencil
- Glue
- Photograph album

INSTRUCTIONS

1 Enlarge the design opposite by 150% on a photocopier. (This drawing is a mirror image of the finished design, as the bonding web pieces are reversed once they are fused in place.)

2 Lay the bonding web, paper side up, over the design and trace the lines in pencil. Write in the numbers so that you'll know which piece is which when you're choosing your fabrics. Cut all the pieces out carefully along the marked lines.

3 Decide which fabric is going where on your design. I used the same fabric in the central panel on each side, then twinned the top left and bottom right corners, and the top right and bottom left corners, but kept the four small hearts all in the same fabric. I then chose a new fabric for the central panel, and a different fabric again for the large heart.

4 Once you've decided which fabric is going where, fuse the appropriate bonding web piece(s) onto the wrong sides of the fabrics with a warm iron. Cut all the shapes out carefully around the edges of the bonding web shapes.

5 Peel off the backing papers and assemble the pieces like a jigsaw puzzle on the piece of interfacing (**a**). Fuse them into position with a warm iron, making sure that they don't move as you press them. Trim the interfacing shape to the edges of the patches (**b**).

a

b

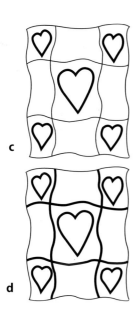

6 Lay a piece of bias binding round the edge of one heart shape, cutting it to length and tucking the raw ends under to neaten them. Fuse the binding in position with a warm iron. Set your machine to a small zigzag and thread it with the blue thread; stitch round each edge of the bias binding. Do the same with all the other heart shapes (**c**).

7 Lay strips of bias binding along the four internal wiggly lines that divide the panels; fuse and stitch them in place as before (**d**).

8 Fuse and stitch a line of bias binding all round the edge of the wiggly rectangle to complete the design (**e**).

9 Lay the shape down on the front of the photograph album and trace round the edge. Spread a generous amount of glue inside this shape, making sure you go right out to the corners, and allow it to dry until it's just tacky; then lay the appliqué shape in position and put a heavy weight on it until the glue is completely dry. (Applying the glue to the album and letting it go tacky helps to prevent it from seeping through the design.)

Africa

Apart from Egypt, my experience of Africa is confined to Tunisia, a country of strange contradictions. An Islamic country where alcohol is freely available; a Mediterranean country in the fertile sections bordering the sea, which seems to become more traditionally African as you travel further south. We took a trip down through the country, passing across the salt flats, and pausing at an oasis where we were deafened by bullfrogs in the water and made friends with a staring-eyed chameleon. We visited the troglodyte villages (where, in a fantastic mixture of past and future, some of the *Star Wars* scenes were shot), and travelled down to the edge of the Sahara.

As we sat at the edge of the desert, staring across the dunes, we sifted sand as fine as flour through our fingers and were introduced to a fennec (a kind of desert fox) cub. The rest of Africa seemed both tantalisingly close and a world away – particularly the Africa of safaris, watering-holes and jungles, which is the 'traditional' aspect of the continent I've chosen to pick up for this section's first project. And I've returned to Egypt – with a slight twist – for the second project.

Zebra quilt

SAFARI FABRICS and animal prints have been very trendy in the fashion world for the past few years, and this trend has spilled over into the world of stitched textiles too. This quilt is my response; a giant 'zebra-hide' created from black and white fabrics, which looks very dramatic hanging on a bright wall; the uneven bottom edge helps create the concept of an animal skin. The shapes are big and bold, and are cut out with pinking shears then appliquéd by machine; choose varied fabrics that have an African feel to them – animal prints, bold tribal patterns, rough textures.

Finished size *80x50in (204x127cm)*

Stitching guide A very quick way to create a large, dramatic wall quilt, as you don't need to neaten the edges of the appliqué pieces. Choose a firm, flat wadding such as Just Like Wool or Needle Punch so that the quilt isn't too squashy; this also helps avoid distortion across the quilt while you're stitching, and means that it will roll up easily under the arm of your machine.

MATERIALS
- Two pieces of white cotton sheeting 80x50in (204x127cm)
- One strip of white cotton sheeting 50x4in (127x10cm)
- One piece of firm wadding 80x50in (204x127cm)
- ½yd (50cm) pieces of various black-and-white cotton prints; you'll need 6-7yd (6-7m) in total
- Black and white sewing threads
- 8yd (8m) black bias binding, ½in (12mm) when folded
- Pencil and black felt pen
- Dressmakers' tracing paper

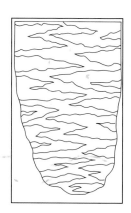

a

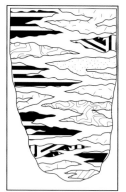

b

c

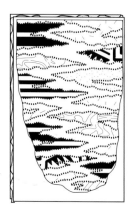

d

1 Tape several pieces of tracing paper together until you have a piece at least 80x50in (204x127cm). Draw a grid of 10in (25cm) squares across the paper, 8 squares by 5.

2 Follow the drawing opposite to copy the solid lines of the design onto the tracing paper, using the grid as a guideline and enlarging the design as you go. Write in the numbers as marked. Go over the lines with black felt pen to make them stronger.

3 Press one of the pieces of white fabric and lay it over the enlarged drawing; draw the lines onto the white fabric in pencil (**a**).

4 Cut out the numbered pieces from the tracing and use these as templates for cutting patches from the black and white fabrics; remember to put the templates right side up on the right side of the fabric, and cut the pieces out with pinking shears. (Cut the fabric pieces just larger than the templates; this will make sure that they will cover the pencil lines on the white background.) Pin the pieces in position on the white fabric (**b**).

5 Press the other piece of white fabric and lay it, right side down, on a flat surface. Cover it with the piece of wadding, then lay the marked white fabric, right side up, on top (**c**). Use your favourite method (tacking, tack gun, safety pins etc) to secure the layers together.

6 Thread your machine with black thread and set it to a medium-width zigzag, then stitch round the edges of the black-and-white patches (**d**) – you don't need to stitch down the straight sides of the pieces; these will be secured in the binding.

7 Unfold one edge of the bias binding and pin it on the front of the quilt, matching the raw edges along the straight sides and curving the binding to match the marked wiggly edge at the bottom of the quilt. Stitch along the fold line with machine straight stitch.

8 Trim away the excess fabric and wadding from the bottom of the quilt by cutting outside the marked wiggly line. Fold the binding over to the back of the quilt and stitch it in place by hand or machine (**e**).

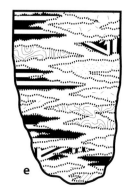

e

9 Fold under a small double hem on all sides of the casing strip of white fabric, and stitch by machine. Pin the strip in position at the top of the quilt back, then slipstitch the top and bottom edges to creating the casing; slip a pole through the casing to hang the quilt.

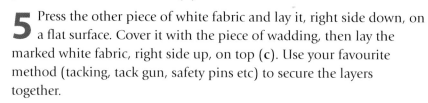
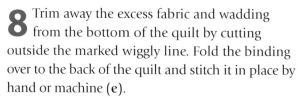

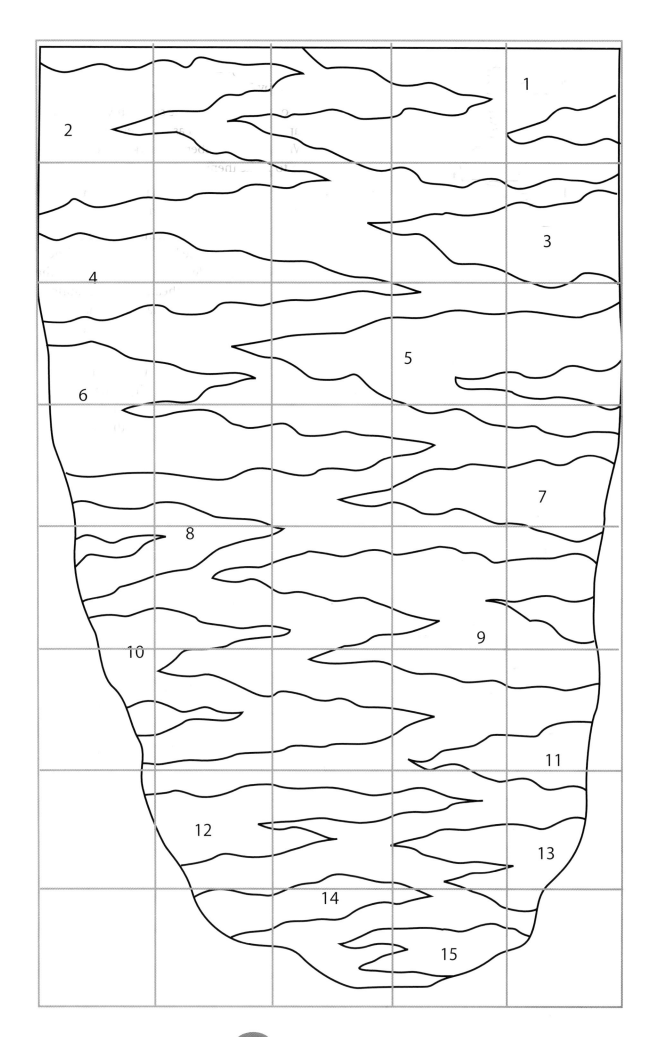

Egyptian wall-hanging

WHEN I WAS A TEENAGER I visited the Treasures of Tutankhamen exhibition in London. Although it was very crowded and we were moved on quickly from room to room by the security guards, the splendour and beauty of the artefacts, spotlit in the darkened rooms, was breathtaking. What I didn't realise was how few of King Tut's treasures were actually shown in that exhibition. 15 years later I slipped in to the Cairo Museum near the end of the day, when there were almost no visitors, and could linger to my heart's content in room upon room stuffed with priceless jewellery, tomb furniture and solid gold sarcophagi. Magical.

When we think of the colours of Egypt, we tend to conjure up the colours of Tutankhamen – gold, turquoise, coral, and lapis lazuli blue. But there's a softer side to Egyptian art, too. When the painter Bridget Riley (who became known for her black and white op art in the 1960s) visited the country, she was intrigued by the paintings which had been preserved for thousands of years on the walls of some of the tombs. She realised that the ancient Egyptians could portray all of their everyday life using shades of just four colours: brown/beige for earth, wood and skin; yellow for sand and the sun; grey-green for plants, and a purply-blue for water and sky.

I decided to use this softer colourscheme for my Egyptian project, creating the design from squares which I put 'on point' to give just an echo of the pyramids. Long stitches in soft textured threads, and beads in wood and other matt finishes, complete the hanging.

Finished size *27x8in (69x20cm)*

Stitching guide Another variation of good old 'rough-edge appliqué' – the squares are deliberately allowed to fray, which makes this a very quick and easy piece to stitch. Choose fabrics with soft colours and finishes, and with a wide variety of textures; I've used linens, slubbed silks, hessian, dyed gauze and imitation suede as well as cottons, and I picked a woven brocade for the background to give a little bit of mystique.

MATERIALS

- One piece of firm yellow ochre background fabric 30x10in (76x25cm)
- One piece of iron-on interfacing 27x8in (69x20cm)
- Assorted matt fabrics in shades of brown, beige, grey-green and purply-blue
- Mixed matt embroidery threads in toning colours; I've used soft cottons and space-dyed slubbed cotton threads
- Yellow sewing thread
- Assorted long beads in toning colours, plus sewing threads to match
- Two hanging rods with at least 8in (20cm) of hanging width

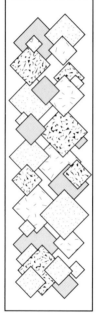

a

1 From your appliqué fabrics, cut squares of different sizes; my largest pieces are 3½in (9cm) square, and the smallest 1in (2.5cm) square. Deliberately fray the edges of some of the squares if they look too neat.

2 Fold under and stitch a small double hem down each long side of the yellow ochre background fabric. Fold under ¼in (5mm) along each short edge and stitch.

3 Lay your square patches 'on point' on the background, overlapping them in different ways (a), and moving them around until the colours, textures and shapes balance well. Cut more patches or discard some if necessary. Leave an inch (2.5cm) of the background fabric free at the top and bottom of the hanging, as this will be wrapped around the hanging rods. Once you're happy with the arrangement, pin the squares in place.

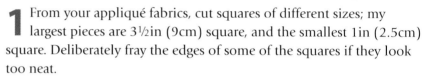

b

c

4 Use long, straight stitches to secure the different squares, working them diagonally across the background so that they are parallel with the edges of the squares (b). Keep varying the threads you're using and the length of your stitches, and overlap the stitches in different directions (c). Use a large, sharp embroidery needle to make sure that you can pull the thread through the layers easily. Work stitches all across the design in this way, until all the squares are secured and there is an even texture of embroidery stitches across the hanging.

5 Scatter the beads across the design and stitch them into place, again attaching them diagonally so that they echo the lines of the stitches and the edges of the squares.

6 Fold the top of the background fabric over one of the hanging rods and slipstitch it into place (d); do the same at the bottom with the other hanging rod.

d

The
Mediterranean

Mediterranean. To someone like me, living in a country which is starved of hot sun for most of the year, even the word is enough to conjure up images of sun-drenched beaches, terracotta tiles, azure seas and leisurely meals during balmy evenings. I've been fortunate enough to visit many different places around the Mediterranean, including spending several years in Malta when I was a child, and I've loved them all.

Of course the different countries in this region have their own very individual identities, not to mention languages (speaking as someone who bought a book called *The Traveller's Guide to Serbo-Croat* before a trip to the former Yugoslavia). But there are many things that unite them too; excellent food, good wine, and a relaxed approach to life that's both frustrating and appealing to people brought up in more uptight countries. You also see many of the same decorative motifs popping up in different guises all over this region, which is why I've grouped them for the purposes of this book. Enjoy a taste of the sun in this section.

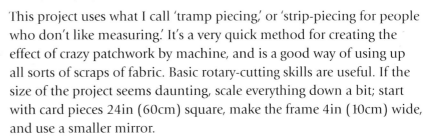

Mosaic mirror

WHEN I DESIGNED and stitched this over-the-top mirror frame, inspired by the work of Spanish designer Antoni Gaudi, I hadn't actually visited his showcase city, Barcelona. After a trip there recently, I think that I understated it a bit! I can see why Barcelona attracts so many people – it is a fabulous city, which is more like a piece of performance art than a serious working city. It also makes you realise that, seen in context, Gaudi wasn't even that bizarre. Although his buildings are the jewels in Barcelona's decorative crown, the city is packed with hundreds of other weird and wonderful buildings of all eras – not to mention the buskers and the open-air sculptures, both human and inanimate. So, if you're making a version of this mirror frame, go mad with its decoration: if you're working in the spirit of Gaudi you can't possibly overdo it...

Finished size   *30in (77cm) square*

Stitching guide   This project uses what I call 'tramp piecing,' or 'strip-piecing for people who don't like measuring.' It's a very quick method for creating the effect of crazy patchwork by machine, and is a good way of using up all sorts of scraps of fabric. Basic rotary-cutting skills are useful. If the size of the project seems daunting, scale everything down a bit; start with card pieces 24in (60cm) square, make the frame 4in (10cm) wide, and use a smaller mirror.

- Lots of different fabric scraps in toning colours; I've used shades of green, yellow, cream and gold

- Two pieces of thick card 30in (77cm) square

- One piece of 2oz or 4oz wadding 30in (77cm) square

- One piece of plain backing fabric 30in (77cm) square

- Scraps of braid, ribbon and lace, and assorted beads, in toning colours

- Sewing thread and extra-strong thread (eg buttonhole thread) to match your colourscheme

- One mirror or mirror-tile, at least 15in (38cm) square
- Craft knife
- Heavy masking tape or parcel tape
- Glue
- Two short lengths of cord for hanging loops

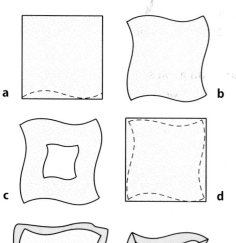

1 On one piece of card, draw a curved line along one edge as shown; make the line smooth and even, so that it curves up for half the length and down for the other half (**a**). (You may want to draw this out on paper first, to get it just right.) When you're happy with the curve, copy it onto the other edges; cut round the lines with a craft knife (**b**).

2 6in (15cm) inside each outer curve, draw an inner curve to echo it. Cut along these lines with the craft knife to make the shape of the frame (**c**). Cut the wadding to the same shape, add a few dabs of glue to the frame and position the wadding on top. Leave until the glue is completely dry.

3 Lay the frame piece on top of the second piece of card and trace round the outside edges only (**d**). Cut round these lines. Lay this piece of card on the background fabric and trim the fabric to 1in (2.5cm) outside the curved shape (**e**). Clip the edges of the fabric, then fold them over the card and glue them in place (**f**).

4 Lay the mirror in the centre of the card shape, so that there's an even border all the way around, and tape it in place along the very edges with the heavy masking tape or parcel tape.

5 Press all your pieces of scrap fabric, then put them in piles. From the largest pieces, cut some straight strips of different widths and set these aside. Cut the others into random strips with your rotary cutter; use a metal rule to ensure that the edges of the strips are straight, but not parallel (**g**).

6 Put random-cut strips of similar length together and join them by machine (**h**); make as many of these units as possible with your scrap fabrics. Press the seams all in the same direction. Cut these new units into random strips at different angles as before (**i**).

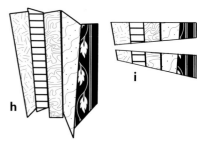

7 Take your straight strips of fabric and use them to make strips of prairie points. (If you don't know how to do these, or want a quick way of creating them, follow the instructions opposite.)

8 Join your new pieced strips to create crazy patchwork units (**j**). Occasionally, slip strips of ribbon or braid into the seams, or add rows of prairie points into the seams so that all the raw edges align.

When the seam is pressed you can either press the prairie points so that the plain points or the folded points are on the right side of the work (**k**); I did a mixture. Join these units into one large piece of patchwork, trimming the edges with the rotary cutter if necessary to make them fit each other well. Keep working in this way until you have a piece several inches larger than your card frame, and press all the seams thoroughly.

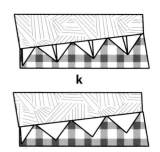

9 Lay the patchwork right side down on a flat surface and lay the padded card piece, wadding side down, on top. Trim the patchwork to within 1in (2.5cm) of the outside edge (don't do the inner edge at this stage), clip the curves, then fold the raw edges of the patchwork over to the back of the card and glue them in place (**l**). Now trim, clip and glue the inner edges in the same way (**m**), clipping carefully into the corners.

10 Scatter beads randomly across the front of the frame then stitch them in place. Lay the padded frame piece over the mirror section, then slipstitch the two shapes together around the outside edges with strong thread. Add loops of cord to two corners to act as hanging loops (**n**); make sure that you stitch them on strongly, as the mirror will be quite heavy by this time.

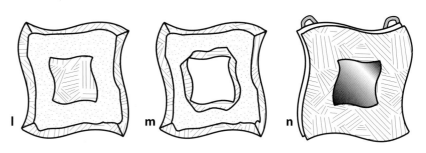

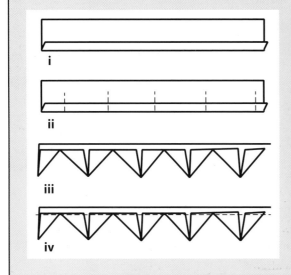

Tip for making quick prairie points

Fold one edge of each strip under by ½in (12mm) and press (**i**). Make cuts along the folded edge of each strip at even intervals (**ii**). Make the cuts twice as far apart as they are deep – so, for instance, on a wide strip make cuts 2in (5cm) deep and 4in (10cm) apart; on a narrow strip make cuts 1in (2.5cm) deep and 2in (5cm) apart. At each side of each cut, make a diagonal fold in the fabric as shown (**iii**). Stitch a line of machine straight stitch just over the raw edges of the triangles to secure them (**iv**).

Sailing boat

THE SIMPLE LINES of this boat design were adapted from a cloisonné plate that was hanging in our apartment on the tiny Greek island of Paros; we'd retreated there to celebrate our 20th wedding anniversary. We've visited several Mediterranean islands over the years, and my memories are always associated with clear blue seas; a sailing boat seemed just the right image to capture both the region and its folk art. To make the patches easy to work with, I've simplified the lines and stylised the shapes, then used coton à broder to appliqué the patches.

Finished size   *15x17in (38x44cm)*

Stitching guide   Another very straightforward project, which you can create in an hour or two. Try and choose fabrics that enhance the design; I used striped fabric for the sails, cutting the patches at an angle to get the stripes parallel with the bottoms of the sails, and I had an offcut of water-patterned furnishing fabric that was perfect for the sea.

MATERIALS
- One piece of pale blue background fabric 15x17in (38x44cm)
- One piece of 'watery' sea fabric 15x6in (38x15cm)
- One piece of mottled brown fabric 8x4in (20x10cm)
- One piece of dark brown fabric 10x4in (25x10cm)
- Large scraps of yellow, tan and bright striped fabrics
- One piece of lightweight iron-on interfacing 24in (60cm) square

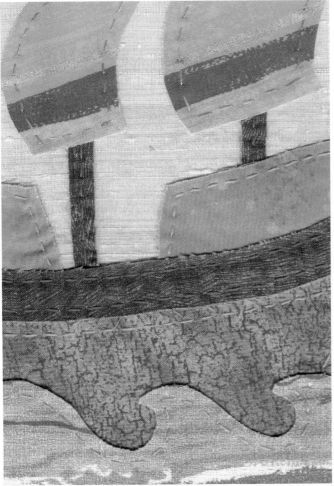

- Coton à border in blue, brown, yellow, tan and a colour to match your striped fabric
- Pencil and paper
- Frame with an aperture roughly 13x15in (33x38cm)

1 Cut pieces of interfacing to fit all your fabrics except the pale blue background, and iron the interfacing pieces onto the backs of your fabrics.

2 Trace or photocopy the templates below and on pages 78 and 79. Use template A to cut a boat shape from the brown mottled fabric, templates B, C, D, E and F to cut masts and the boat rim from the dark brown fabric, templates G and H to cut cabins from the tan fabric, templates I, J, K and L to cut small sails from the yellow fabric, and templates M, N, O, P and Q to cut main sails from the striped fabric. Remember to put the templates right side up on the front of the fabric.

3 Press the pale blue background fabric and lay it on a flat surface. Lay the main boat piece on the background so that its bottom is about 4in (10cm) from the bottom of the background fabric and its right-hand side is about 3in (8cm) from the right edge of the background fabric. Lay the masts in place (**a**), and pin all these patches in position. Stitch down the centre of each mast piece using long running stitches in brown coton à broder (**b**).

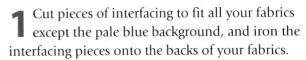

B

C

4 Lay the cabin pieces at the top of the boat section, then add the boat rim so that it overlaps the top of the boat and the bottom of the cabin. Work a line of running stitches in brown all round the boat rim, just in from the raw edges (**c**). Now use tan coton à broder to stitch along the sides and top edges of the cabins (**d**).

5 Pin all the sails in position on the masts (note that the small sail on the right overlaps one of the main sails), then appliqué all the sails (**e**) using coton à broder in the appropriate colour.

6 Cut the top edge of your 'sea' rectangle into stylised wave shapes (**f**) – copy the ones in the picture, or create your own. (You may want to draw the shapes out on paper before you cut into your fabric.) Pin this section onto the picture so that the waves overlap the bottom of the boat, and stitch in blue along the wavy edge (**g**). Now stitch in tan round the sides and top edge of the boat section (**h**). Press the picture from the back, and it's ready to mount in your frame.

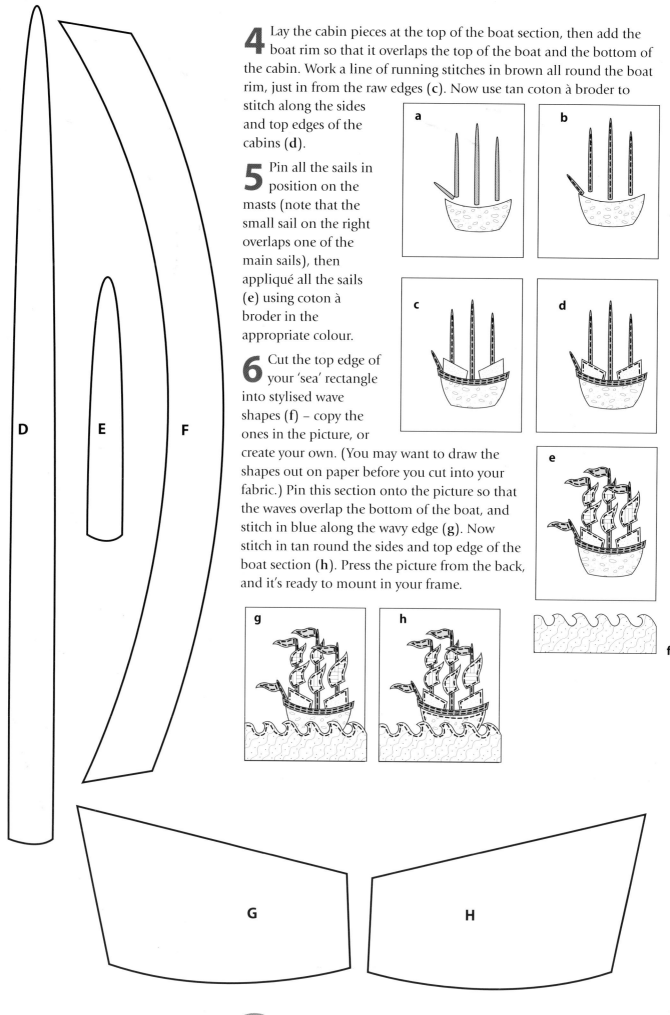

Shadow-quilting tablecloth

ALL OVER THE MEDITERRANEAN, you can find evidence of ancient occupations – Etruscan, Minoan, Carthaginian, ancient Greek, and especially Roman. Sometimes these civilisations developed distinctive decorative motifs to embellish their pottery and metalwork, floors and walls – for instance the strange stylised squid/octopus motifs used on Minoan pottery – but many others were borrowed from each other, adapted and re-used until it's almost impossible to tell them apart. The spade-shaped motifs I've used here are perfect examples of this trend. I've made them into a shadow-quilted tablecloth, worked in a Mediterranean colourscheme of mottled terracottas, yellows, creams and browns, but of course you could adapt the colours to suit your own decor.

Finished size   *I've worked on a 70in (180cm) diameter tablecloth*

Stitching guide   The secret of success with this design is careful preparation and measuring; once the pieces are in position under the muslin, the stitching is very straightforward. To make sure that the patches don't move out of position while you're doing the quilting, they're fused onto the tablecloth with lightweight bonding web.

MATERIALS

- One circular cream tablecloth 70in (180cm) in diameter
- Circle of cream muslin 36in (92cm) in diameter
- Red cotton fabric 16in (40cm) square
- Dark yellow cotton fabric 12in (30cm) square
- Dark orange cotton fabric 7x4in (18x10cm)
- Bright orange cotton fabric 9in (23cm) square
- Brown cotton fabric 5in (13cm) square
- 10-11yd (10-11m) cream upholstery braid
- Cream sewing thread, plus sewing or quilting threads in red, dark orange, bright orange, dark yellow and brown
- Thin card
- Chalk marker
- Pencil and paper if you're tracing rather than photocopying the templates
- ½yd (50cm) Bondaweb or Heat 'n' Bond

INSTRUCTIONS

1 Lay the bonding web over the templates on page 83 and trace four large spade shapes (**A**), four small spade shapes (**B**), four sets of diamond-and-teardrop shapes (**C**), four smaller diamonds (**D**), four bobbin shapes (**E**), and 20 circles (**F**). Cut out roughly each spade piece and each set of smaller templates, leaving a small margin of web around the lines. (Leave the sets of smaller shapes on the same piece of bonding web; you don't need to cut them out individually.)

2 Fuse the web side of each bonding web shape onto the back of the appropriate fabric. Fuse the A shapes onto the red fabric, the B shapes onto the bright orange fabric, the C and D shapes onto the yellow fabric, the E shapes onto the dark orange, and the F circles onto the brown. Cut each piece out carefully along the marked lines.

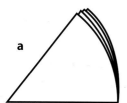

3 Fold the tablecloth accurately into eight segments (**a**) and press the folds firmly; open it and lay it on a flat surface. From the centre, measure out 12in (30cm) along each fold and mark the position with a pin (**b**). Use the chalk marker to join the points marked by the pins, to create a circle (**c**).

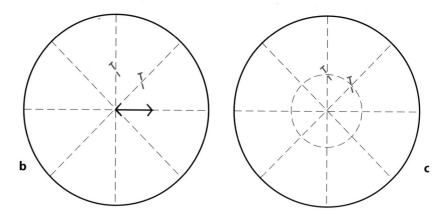

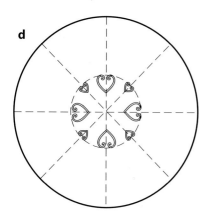

4 Peel the backing paper off each piece as you lay out the design during this stage. Lay large and small spade shapes alternately round the chalk circle, so that the outside curves of the hearts are on the chalk line and the points are on the folds (**d**). Fuse these pieces into position with a warm iron. Position a bobbin shape inside each large spade shape, with two circles outside it (**e**); then fuse a set of diamond-and-teardrop shapes inside each large spade (**f**). Fuse a small diamond inside each small spade shape and a circle outside it (**g**).

Finally, fuse the other circles at even spaces between the spade shapes (**h**) – use the folds to help you position them. Once all the pieces are fused firmly in place, press the cloth to remove the folds.

5 Fold the circle of muslin accurately into eight segments and press. On each straight edge, measure out 15in

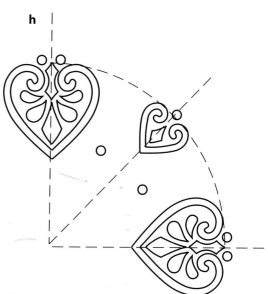

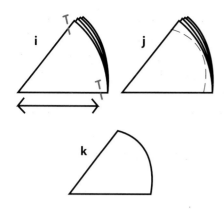

(38cm) from the centre and mark with a pin (**i**). Use the chalk marker to draw a smooth curve joining the marked points (**j**), then cut through all the layers along this line (**k**). Unfold the circle, press out the folds, then neaten the scalloped edges with the upholstery braid (it's important to do this straight away so that the muslin doesn't fray too much). I did this by going round the edge with a medium zigzag stitch in cream, then laying the braid over the stitching and appliquéing it with another line of zigzag over the top.

6 Lay the decorated cloth, right side up, on a flat surface, then lay the circle of muslin over the top, right side up, so that the centres of the circles align. Tack the two layers together, running the lines of tacking around and between the fused patches.

7 Stitch round each coloured patch just outside its edges; match the threads to the patches, and use a small, even running stitch. When all the patches have been stitched, remove the tacking threads.

Fleur-de-lys breadcloth

THE FLEUR-DE-LYS (a stylised lily motif) also appears in many Mediterranean countries, but is particularly associated with France. It also crops up in many heraldic devices, so I thought I'd interpret it in gold for this design. A breadcloth is a practical way of keeping oven-warmed bread or rolls hot for longer, but a cloth like this is a pretty way of showing off fancy breads or cakes even if they're cold, too! I've kept things easy and used thick damask table napkins as my foundation fabric; you get the luxurious feel and texture of the damask without having to bother about turning under the edges.

Finished size *I used 17in (43cm) square napkins, but this design would work on any size*

Stitching guide Definitely the quickest design in this book; bonding web neatens the edges of the silk, and the machine stitching can be done in a trice. A perfect machine appliqué project for a beginner.

MATERIALS
- Two damask table napkins
- Gold silk dupion 10in (25cm) square
- Bondaweb or Heat 'n' Bond 10in (25cm) square
- Metallic gold machine-stitching thread
- Sewing thread to match your napkins
- Square of firm, flat wadding ½in (12mm) smaller in each direction than your napkin
- Pencil

INSTRUCTIONS

1 Trace the fleur-de-lys design opposite four times onto the paper side of the bonding web (**a**), then lay the tracings web side down on the back of the silk fabric and fuse into position (**b**). Cut the shapes out along the traced lines.

a

b

c

d

2 Lay one of the napkins right side up on a flat surface. Peel the backing paper off the motifs and position them right side up on the napkin, one in each corner (**c**). Check that all the motifs are the same distance from the napkin corners, then fuse them in position.

3 Lay the second napkin, right side down, on a flat surface and position the wadding on top so that there's an even border of fabric all round. Lay the second napkin on top, right side up, and pin the layers together (**d**).

4 Thread your machine with sewing thread to match the damask and stitch a line of straight stitch or small zigzag just inside each edge of the square, so that the wadding is sealed between the two layers of damask.

5 Re-thread your machine with the gold thread and set it to a medium zigzag; stitch round the edge of each fleur-de-lys motif. This appliqués and quilts each motif at the same time.

Scandinavia

This is part of the world I've never been to, although I would love to see it – particularly the fjords. Some friends spent one summer cruising the Norwegian coast free because the husband was part of the ship's entertainment crew: nice work if you can get it, but I don't think my skills with comb and paper are going to take me in that direction. I'm sure the scenery in Scandinavia isn't all mountains, fjords and pine forests, but it's nice to picture it like that – particularly for we Brits, whose country is noticeably lacking in the department of mountains and fjords, even though we're just across the water.

❄❄❄❄❄❄❄❄❄❄❄❄❄❄❄❄❄❄❄❄❄❄

Christmas cards

I PARTICULARLY LOVE the wonderful Christmas decorations and traditions that Scandinavian countries have; I think that Garrison Keillor's piece *Nu Er Der Jul Igen* is one of the most captivating things I've ever read. Maybe I'm looking through rose-tinted spectacles, but it seems that, amid all the present-giving and over-eating, the Christmas traditions in Scandinavia have managed to keep a sense of what the central Christmas story is all about. So I've chosen three Christmas cards as my first Scandinavian projects; these are all quick and easy, but you can embellish them with beads, sequins, glitter glue etc to your heart's content.

Finished size *Tree design 6x8in (15x20cm); snowflake design 6x8in (15x20cm); stocking design 4½x7in (11.5x18cm)*

Stitching guide I've used machine cutwork for these designs; if you're au fait with machine satin stitch you'll find them a doddle. If it's your first try at this technique, begin with the stocking, as it's the easiest shape – and don't stint on the foundation paper; that's what stops the fabric from distorting as you stitch. I've given the basic colours for the fabrics; pick ones with Christmassy prints on them if you can to echo the seasonal theme.

MATERIALS

- One piece of navy blue fabric 6x8in (15x20cm)
- One piece of pale blue fabric 6x8in (15x20cm)
- Two pieces of green fabric, one 4½x7in (11.5x18cm) and one 5in (13cm) square
- One piece of red fabric 5in (13cm) square
- One piece of opalescent fabric 5in (13cm) square
- Three pieces of firm, flat wadding 5in (13cm) square
- Three pieces of Stitch 'n' Tear or cartridge paper
- One cream card blank with an oval aperture 4½x6in (11.5x15cm)
- One white card blank with a rectangular aperture 4x6in (10x15cm)
- One red card blank with an arched aperture 3x5½in (8x14cm)
- Scraps of braid, lace, sequins, beads, Christmassy buttons etc to decorate

- Red, green and silver machine sewing thread
- Pencil
- Paper and thin card, or template plastic
- Stick glue

INSTRUCTIONS

1 Trace or photocopy the three large shapes below and opposite, then transfer them to thin card and cut them out (or trace them onto template plastic and cut them out). Trace the tree template (**A**) onto the front of the square of green fabric, the stocking template (**B**) onto the front of the red fabric, and the snowflake template (**C**) onto the front of the opalescent fabric.

2 Lay one piece of Stitch 'n' Tear or cartridge paper on a flat surface and cover with a square of wadding; lay the red fabric, right side up, on top, and pin the layers together. Do the same with the square of green fabric, and then with the square of opalescent fabric. (If your opalescent fabric frays badly, back it with a layer of thin iron-on interfacing before you do this bit.)

3 Thread your machine with red thread and set it to a medium-width satin stitch, and stitch all the way around the marked stocking outline on the red fabric. Do the same in green around the tree, and in silver round the snowflake.

4 Pull the foundation paper away from the back of each design, then carefully cut round the stitched shapes, just outside the line of satin stitching so that you don't cut the stitches.

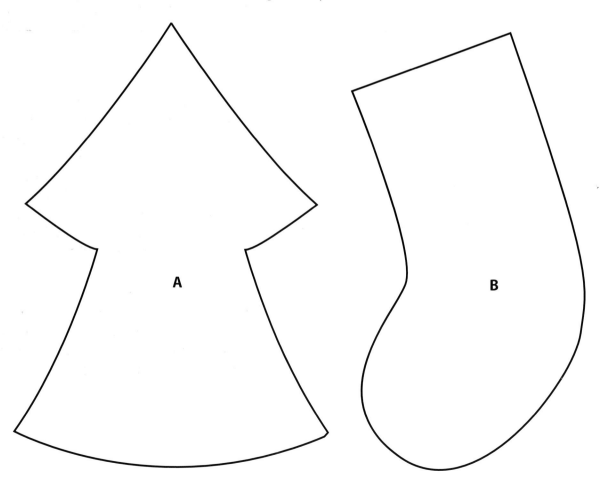

Instructions for mounting card designs

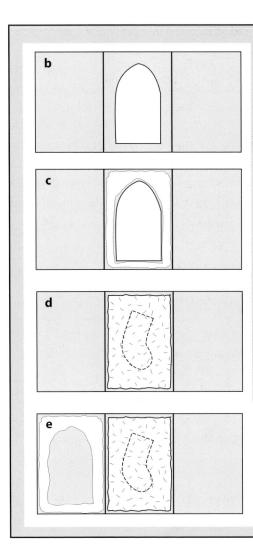

Try the design in the aperture of the card it will go in, then trim away excess background fabric until the whole design is just smaller than the folded card blank (**a**).

Open up the card blank and lay it face down on a flat surface (**b**). Spread some glue around the edges of the central section, right up to the edge of the aperture (**c**), then carefully position the design in the centre (**d**), right side down, checking its position from the front.

Smooth the background fabric out across the glued section so that it lies flat. Spread some glue round the edges of the left-hand flap (**e**); don't glue it all over in case the glue migrates through the design.

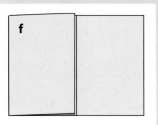

Fold the flap over the back of the design (**f**), then put the card under a couple of heavy books until the glue is completely dry.

5 Pin the snowflake in the centre of the pale blue fabric, the tree in the centre of the dark blue fabric, and the stocking on the remaining piece of green fabric. Stitch them in place invisibly by taking a few stitches from the back of the work into the wadding on the padded motifs, stitching just inside the edges (this allows the edges of the motifs to peep out of the card apertures). Use the braid, sequins, beads etc to decorate the designs as you wish.

6 Follow the instructions above to mount the tree card in the oval card blank, the stocking card in the red card blank, and the snowflake card in the white card blank. The edges of the cutwork motifs will just peep out from the edges of the apertures.

Table ribbons

I'M RATHER TAKEN by the ribbons which Scandinavians sometimes use to decorate the table on festive occasions, so I've designed my own for this section. The ribbons are stretched across the table from side to side and pinned in place, acting like narrow table runners; you could also pin them along the long edges of a buffet table for a Christmas feast. The ribbons are very quick to make, but if you prefer a smaller project you could make one up as a cake ribbon; in this case, make it about 1in (2.5cm) longer than your cake's circumference, position it round the cake once it's iced, and pin the ends over each other.

Finished size   *My narrowest ribbon is 1½in (4cm); the widest is 4in (10cm) wide*

Stitching guide   A very quick way of making a festive table look great, and it doesn't have to be limited to Christmas; choose ribbons in appropriate colours for birthdays, new baby celebrations, weddings and anniversaries.

MATERIALS
- Strips of Christmas fabric or ribbon
- Lengths of lace, fancy edging, braid, broderie anglaise etc (remember that if you want to edge both sides of your ribbon you'll need twice the ribbon's length)
- Scraps of Christmas fabric
- Scraps of bonding web
- Glitter glue, sequins, beads etc to decorate

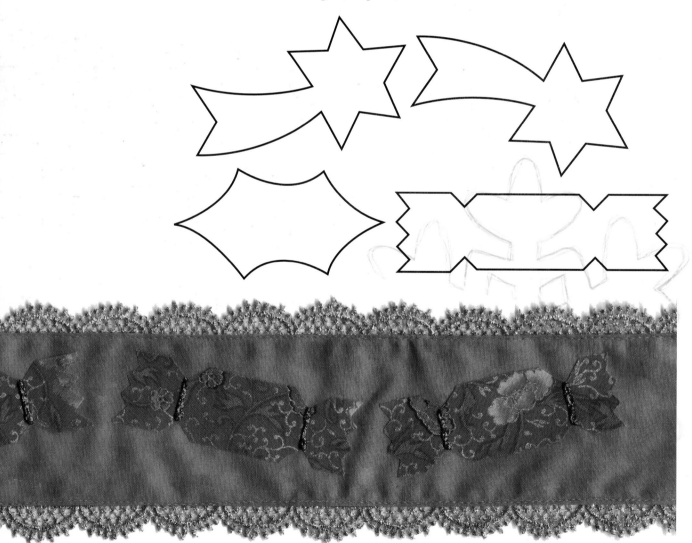

INSTRUCTIONS

1 Cut a strip of Christmas fabric or ribbon the required length plus 2in (5cm); if you're using fabric, cut the strip ½in (12mm) wider than your finished width, then press under and stitch a ¼in (5mm) hem each side.

2 If you're using appliqué on your ribbon, choose your motif from the ones on page 92. Trace the motif onto the paper side of the bonding web, then fuse the web to the back of scraps of Christmas fabric. Cut out the motifs along the marked lines, then lay them web side down along the ribbon or fabric strip; fuse them into place with a warm iron.

3 If you're building up the design in layers of ribbon, braid, lace etc, try out different combinations until you're happy with the design, then stitch the layers together by hand or machine.

4 Finish the outside edges of your ribbon as you wish, with strips of braid, lace, broderie anglaise etc. Finally, add any glitter glue details, beads or sequins.

Arctic & Antarctic

Maybe you're wondering what could possibly be inspirational about the frozen wastes of the far north or the far south – or maybe you're one of those people who longs to spend months in a field station on an ice floe, observing penguins or polar bears. I'm a great armchair traveller to the top and the bottom of the world; when I was doing one hand-sewing project, I spent hours entranced by Ranulph Fiennes (surely part of the world's insane heritage of obsessive explorers) reading his book about travelling to the North Pole. (I later also read Mike Stroud's book about the same journey for the other side of the story!)

Their world of sastrugi (wind-sculpted ice mountains), fillings being removed from their teeth by frozen Mars Bars, removing each other from ice melts, and marching for days in sub-zero temperatures on empty stomachs because they couldn't agree on who was going to make breakfast, alternately mesmerised and horrified me. I think that maybe I'll just go there in my imagination.

Herb sachets

FOR THESE TWO LITTLE HERB SACHETS I've picked up the cold colours of water and icebergs, using shades of cool blues, jades and mauves offset with white and opalescent fabrics. I've made the crazy patchwork for each of them in the same way, but used more colour in one sachet and more white in another; many of the fabrics also have a slight sheen – silks, satins, brocades and chintzes – which, along with the opalescent beads, catch the light and add to the icy feel.

Finished size *10in (25cm) square*

Stitching guide The crazy patchwork in these sachets is made very quickly by machine, using the same technique as the mirror frame on page 73; basic rotary cutting skills are useful. Stitch up a batch of these sachets in an evening or two, then you've always got a store of little thankyou presents or Christmas gifts.

MATERIALS
- Two pieces of white or pale blue backing fabric 10in (25cm) square
- Four pieces of 2oz polyester wadding 10in (25cm) square
- Large scraps of assorted fabrics in white, opalescent, plus pastel shades of blue, jade and mauve
- Circular opalescent beads in assorted sizes
- Satin bias binding, 1in (2.5cm) when folded, in pale green and pale blue, 45in (115cm) of each colour
- White sewing thread
- Herbs or pot pourri

INSTRUCTIONS

1 Press all your scraps of fabric. Follow the instructions on pages 73 and 74 to create machine-made crazy patchwork, cutting and piecing until you have two pieces of patchwork that you can trim down to 10in (25cm) square.

2 Lay one piece of backing fabric right side down on a flat surface and cover it with one square of wadding. Put a small handful of herbs or pot pourri in the centre of the piece of wadding (**a**), then cover with another square of wadding and then one of the patchwork

a

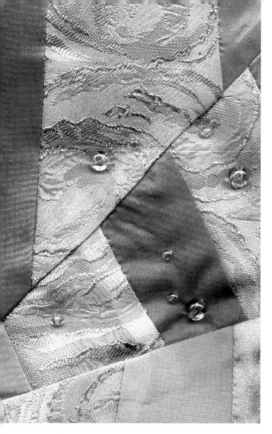

squares, right side up (**b**). Pin or tack all the layers together, then round the corners off evenly with scissors (**c**).

3 Unfold one edge of one piece of binding and pin it around the edges of the patchwork, right sides together, so that the raw edges align (**d**). Fold the raw ends over so that they just butt up to each other. Stitch round the fold line by machine, then fold the binding over to the wrong side and slipstitch it in place; slipstitch the edges together invisibly at the join (**e**).

4 On one or both sachets, stitch the opalescent beads in random positions to decorate the surface of the patchwork.

Aurora borealis mirror

ALTHOUGH (APPARENTLY) you can see the aurora borealis, or northern lights, from Scotland when conditions are right, you need to go up to the Arctic circle to see the spectacle at its best. My dictionary describes it as 'a luminous meteoric phenomenon of electrical character, with a tremulous motion and streamers of light,' which makes it sound rather more like something out of *Close Encounters*, but by all accounts it's one of the great wonders of the natural world. My mother bought me this piece of fabric from America; it's one of Mickey Lawler's handpainted Skydyes, and it was so beautiful I couldn't bear to cut it up, so I designed this mirror frame so that I could quilt it in one piece.

Finished size *20x16in (51x41cm)*

Stitching guide I've used contour quilting for this project – the simplest quilting technique there is, as you just follow the lines that are already on a printed, painted or textured fabric. You can do the quilting by hand or machine, whichever you prefer.

MATERIALS
- Thick card: two pieces 20x16in (51x41cm), one piece 18½x14½in (47x37cm)
- 2oz polyester wadding or similar: one piece 20x16in (51x41cm), one piece 22x18in (56x46cm)
- One piece of printed, dyed or painted fabric 22x18in (56x46cm)
- One piece of white fabric 22x18 (56x46cm)
- One piece of opalescent fabric 22x18in (56x46cm)
- One piece of muslin 22x18in (56x46cm)
- Glue
- Craft knife
- Sewing or quilting thread(s) to tone in with your bright fabric

- Strong white sewing thread
- Mirror or mirror tile roughly 8x12in (20x30cm)
- Heavy masking tape or parcel tape
- 12in (30cm) toning cord for hanging

INSTRUCTIONS

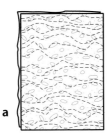

a

1 Lay the muslin down on a flat surface and cover it with the larger piece of wadding. Lay the coloured fabric, right side up, on top of the wadding, then use your favourite method (tacking, tack gun, pins etc) to secure the three layers.

2 Using hand or machine stitching, stitch along the main lines of the pattern or paint areas on the fabric. If the fabric doesn't have strong lines that you can stitch over, simply create a random pattern with your stitching (**a**). Remove any tacking threads etc.

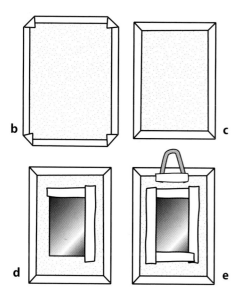

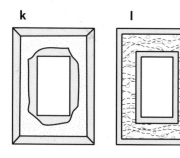

3 Lay the piece of white fabric right side down on a flat surface and position one of the larger pieces of card on top so that there's an even border of fabric all the way around. Fold the corners over and glue them in position (**b**), then fold the edges over and glue them (**c**).

4 Lay the mirror or mirror tile face up on the card so that there's an even border all the way around, then tape it in firmly in position (**d**). Lay the hanging cord in a V shape at the top of the frame and tape the raw ends in position (**e**).

5 On the remaining large piece of card, measure in 5in (13cm) from each edge and carefully cut out the central rectangle with the craft knife to create a frame shape (**f**). On the smaller piece of card, measure in 3½in (9cm) from each edge, then cut out the central rectangle in the same way.

6 Spray or spread a little glue on the larger frame shape and lay the second piece of wadding over the top. When the glue is completely dry, cut away wadding inside the central rectangle to create a padded frame. Lay the opalescent fabric, right side down, on a flat surface and lay the padded frame, wadding side down, on top so that there's an even border of fabric all the way around (**g**). Fold over and glue first the corners and then the sides of the fabric (**h**). Trim the fabric away from the central rectangle to within 2in (5cm) of the card (**i**). Clip just into the corners (**j**), then fold the fabric over the card and glue it in place (**k**).

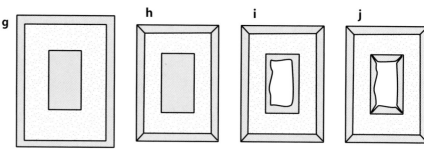

7 Lay the quilted fabric right side down on a flat surface and position the remaining card frame over the top so that there's an even border of fabric all the way around. Glue the corners and sides of the fabric over the card in the same way as before, then trim, clip and glue the central rectangle as before.

8 Lay the opalescent frame right side up on a flat surface. Spray or spread a generous amount of glue on the wrong (card) side of the coloured frame piece, then glue it to the opalescent frame shape so that there are even borders inside and outside (**l**). (If you've used liquid glue rather than spray, wait until it's just tacky before you put the two together so that the glue doesn't leak out under the top frame.)

9 Lay the double frame over the backing card so that the mirror shows through the aperture (**m**). Using the strong white thread, slipstitch the two rectangles together all the way round the edges, taking some extra stitches through the hanging cord when you come to it to give it extra strength.

The British Isles

For such a tiny group of islands, this region of the world has a remarkable heritage of both beautiful art and wonderful textiles. Perhaps it's because our history involves so many different influences, all of which have left their mark artistically – from the mosaic floors laid during the Roman invasion, through the Scandinavian influences that held sway in the north (for a long time Orkney was part of Norway), to the home-grown beauty of Celtic art and design.

And as far as quilting goes, Britain has a heritage probably unrivalled by any other part of the world. Wholecloth quilting, a humble craft born of necessity during cold winters in unheated houses, developed into an art form that still has massive influence today. It was taken over to the New World by the early pioneers, where it had its own transatlantic flowering, but happily the tradition of wholecloth quilting has never quite died out in Britain – though the industrial revolution came perilously close to making it obsolete. I've used two developments of wholecloth quilting for the projects in this section.

Celtic herb pillow

A FEW MONTHS BEFORE WRITING this book I had the chance to visit the highlands of Scotland for the first time in 25 years, and they were just as beautiful as I remembered them. During the intervening years there's been a tremendous revival of interest in all things Celtic – not that the Celts were all Scots, by any means, but the Celtic strand is still very strong in Scottish life and tradition. In particular, many

people delight in the complex knots that are the best-known feature of Celtic art; these lend themselves very well indeed to hand quilting, as this project shows.

I've adapted two different knot designs, one square one and one long one, and stitched them in large sashiko stitches (see page 44) using coloured coton à broder; this gives an extra flash of colour to the finished pillow. I've then filled it with a mixture of stuffing and pot pourri, so that it can please several senses at once.

Finished size   *16in (41cm) square*

Stitching guide   This project is suitable for people of all skill levels; the design is quilted using cotons à broder and quite large stitches, so that the colours define the pattern strongly. I've used six different colours of thread for my design, but if you prefer you could use fewer, or stitch the whole design in one colour.

MATERIALS

- Two 17in (43cm) squares of white or cream cotton fabric (lawn, soft calico etc). This fabric should be fairly transparent, as you'll be tracing a design onto it: if you're not sure, lay it over the drawing on page 105: if you can see the lines clearly through it, the fabric is OK!

- One 17in (43cm) square of 2oz polyester wadding, or any other wadding that you prefer

- One 17in (43cm) square of white or cream muslin

- Two 8in (20cm) squares of white or cream muslin for making the inner herb sachet

- Cotons à broder in six different mid-pastel colours (if you are using yellow, choose a rich orangey-yellow to ensure that it shows up on the fabric); one skein of each colour. (If you can't find cotons à broder, you could use stranded embroidery cottons instead.)

- White or cream sewing thread

- Pack of polyester stuffing

- Herbs, spices or pot-pourri to put inside the sachet

- Water-soluble pen

- Paper, pencil and black felt pen if you are tracing rather than photocopying the design

INSTRUCTIONS

1 Trace or photocopy the designs on page 105 and 106; if necessary, go over the designs with a black felt pen to make the lines stronger.

2 Press one of your squares of cotton fabric, then use a long ruler and the water-soluble pen to draw in the diagonals faintly on the fabric (**a**). This will help you position the different parts of the design. Lay one of your squares of cotton fabric over the square knot design so that there's an even border of fabric all around and the corners of the design lie on the marked diagonals; secure the layers with a couple of pins, then trace the lines of the design using the water-soluble pen (**b**). Unpin.

3 Trace one repeat of the long knot design outside each side of the square knot (**c**), using the diagonals to help you keep the distances even. Unpin.

a

b

c

4 Lay the square of muslin on a flat surface, cover it with the square of wadding, then lay the marked design, right side up, on top of the wadding. Secure the three layers together with a couple of lines of tacking in each direction.

5 Using the coton à broder, quilt each element of the design in a different colour; quilt using quite long running stitches, with each stitch about twice as long on the front as it is on the back, and make sure you go through all three layers. (If you're using stranded cottons, use three strands in the needle at one time.)

6 When the design is complete, remove the tacking and spray the front with cold water to remove the pen lines. Allow the fabric to dry completely.

7 Put the two pieces of cotton fabric right sides together and stitch a half-inch (12mm) seam round the edges by machine; leave a gap of about 4in (10cm) in the centre of one side for turning (**d**). Clip the corners, trim the wadding back to the seam line on all four sides, and turn out. Press the very edges of the square to set the seams, and press under the seam allowances on the open edge.

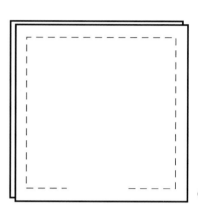

d

8 Make a small square bag by stitching the two squares of muslin together round the edges, leaving a small opening for the pot pourri/herbs (**e**). Insert the pot pourri, then stitch the opening closed (**f**).

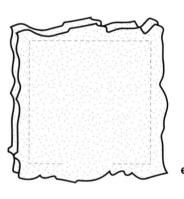

e

9 Stuff the pillow gently with the stuffing, then make a hole in the centre with your fingers and slip the muslin sachet into the centre of the pillow. This keeps the pot pourri or herbs, which can be slightly greasy, out of contact with the surfaces of the pillow.

10 Slipstitch the open edge closed, then use the remaining cotons à broder to make tassels and stitch them to the corners of the herb pillow.

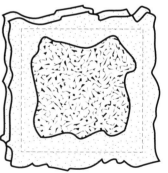

f

Sewing bag and pincushion

I LOVE DOING HAND QUILTING on silk; the needle just seems to slip through the fabric like a knife through butter, and the sheen on the silk sets off the texture of the wholecloth designs as the fabric catches the light. For the sewing bag and pincushion shown here I've chosen a rose pink silk dupion, and decorated the projects with two different sizes of the same simple wholecloth motif.

The little bag is just right for popping bits of hand-sewing in when you know you've got a long journey or a long wait (or both!); the sturdy pincushion has a recess in the rim where you can rest your needle threader, embroidery scissors etc while you're working. The firm wadding used to give texture to the quilting also acts as a lining for the bag, which helps protect the silk from being damaged by the points of scissors and needles.

Finished size   *Bag, 11x16in (28x41cm); pincushion, to fit a pad 4½in (11.5cm) in diameter*

Stitching guide   Although these projects are hand quilted, the motifs are very simple and will take you hardly any time to stitch. Don't feel you have to use silk; cotton fabric would work just as well for both projects, but choose a plain colour or one with only a tiny pattern so that the quilted design doesn't get lost.

MATERIALS
- Rose silk dupion; one piece 44x12in (112x30cm) for the bag, two pieces 11x3in (28x7.5cm) for the casings, one piece 7in (18cm) square for the pincushion
- Firm, thin wadding; one piece 12x24in (30x60cm), one piece 7in (18cm) square
- Cream quilting thread
- Pink sewing thread
- 1yd (1m) fine cream cord for the drawstring
- White pencil crayon
- Paper, pencil and black felt pen if you're tracing the design rather than photocopying
- One wooden pincushion blank with a circular pad

INSTRUCTIONS

1 Trace or photocopy the flower designs on page 108 and 109; if you're tracing the designs, go over the lines with black felt pen to make them stronger.

2 Fold the large piece of pink fabric in half across its width and press the halfway line to mark it. Unfold it, and lay it right side up over the large flower design so that the bottom of the flower is about 2in (5cm) up from the fold (**a**). Trace the lines of the flower using the white pencil crayon.

3 Fold the wadding in half across its width and press the fold to mark it. Unfold the wadding,

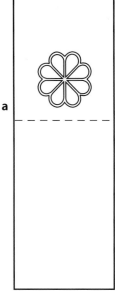

a

lay it on the wrong side of the silk so that the folds align and tack it in place all round the edges of the wadding (**b**).

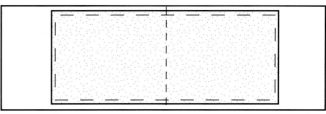

b

4 Quilt the lines of the design using one strand of cream quilting thread. Keep the stitches even in length, and make sure that the curves round the tips of all the petals are smooth.

5 On the strips of pink silk, turn under and press a half-inch (12mm) single hem on all sides. Stitch down the hems on just the short edges.

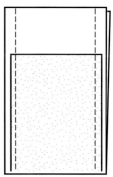

6 Fold the large bag piece in half, right sides together, and stitch a half-inch (12mm) seam down each side (**c**). Clip the bottom corners and trim the raw edges of the silk and wadding to within ¼in (5mm) of the seam line; turn right side out and press the seams.

c

7 At the top of the bag, fold the raw edges of the silk under by ½in (12mm) along the short ends; press. Fold the edges under again by 5in (13cm) and press; the folded edges should now conceal the top edge of the wadding piece. Tack just along this line to secure the layers (**d**).

d

8 On the right side of the bag piece, position one strip so that the bottom edge just covers the line of tacking (**e**). Stitch by machine just inside this edge and the top edge. Do the same with the other strip on the other side of the bag; remove the tacking threads.

e

9 Thread the cord through the casings in a double loop as shown (**f**), then tie the ends to neaten them. (A double loop like this makes a more effective drawstring.)

10 Trace the smaller flower design into the centre of the remaining square of pink silk, using the white pencil crayon as before. Tack this square over the square of wadding, then quilt the design using the cream quilting thread. Remove the tacking threads, and follow the manufacturer's instructions to cover the pincushion pad and secure it in its frame.

f

ACKNOWLEDGEMENTS

Many thanks to the following people, whose help made putting this book together even more of a pleasure:

- Robert Claxton for the photographs on pages 16, 25, 28, 32, 38, 39, 48, 56, 64, 68, 72, 74, 78, 96, 99, 102 and 103

- Colin and Judy Frampton, and Brian and Louise Comb, for letting us take over their houses and gardens for photography

- Angela Besley, for lending us the San Blas cat to photograph

- All the staff at CPO, for their unfailing help and support on Teamwork Craftbooks titles

BOOK LIST

As I was doing the research for *A Trip Around the World*, I found the following books helpful and fascinating; if this book has whetted your appetite for exploring the world's decorative arts you may like them too. Some of them are reprints of pattern books of decorative designs first published in the 19th or early 20th centuries, Dover books are also very useful sources of inspiration, as are the series of Celtic design books written by Aidan Meehan and published by Thames & Hudson.

- *Border Designs* Stephen Astley, Studio Editions 1990 (ISBN 1 85170 381 0)

- *Celtic Art* George Bain, Constable 1992 (ISBN 0 09 461830 5)

- *Celtic Knotwork* Iain Bain, Constable 1986 (ISBN 0 09 4698 10 4)

- *Decorative Patterns of the Ancient World* Flinders Petrie, Studio Editions 1990 (ISBN 1 85170 359 4)

- *Embroidery* Mary Gostelow, Marshall Cavendish Editions 1977

- *The Encyclopaedia of Patterns and Motifs* Dorothy Bosomworth, Studio 1995 (ISBN 1 85891 221 0)

- *The History of Ornament, Antiquity to Modern Times* Alexander Speltz, Studio Editions 1989 (ISBN 1 85170 175 3)

- *Meyer's Handbook of Ornament* Franz Meyer, Omega Books 1987 (ISBN 1 85007 038 5)

- *Pattern Designing* Archibald Christie, The Clarendon Press, first edition 1910

- *The Treasury of Ornament* Heinrich Dolmetsch, Studio Editions 1989 (ISBN 1 85170 176 1)

- *World Textiles* John Gillow and Bryan Sentance, Thames & Hudson 1999 (ISBN 0 500 01950 9)

- *376 Decorative Allover Patterns from Historic Tilework and Textiles* Charles Cahier and Arthur Martin, Dover 1989 (ISBN 0 486 26146 8)